THE BODY IMAGE TRAP

THE BODY IMAGE TRAP
Understanding and rejecting body image myths

Marion Crook, B.Sc.N

Self-Counsel Press
(a division of)
International Self-Counsel Press Ltd.
Canada   U.S.A.

Printed in Canada

First edition: December, 1991

Canadian Cataloguing in Publication Data

Crook, Marion, 1941 -
   The body image trap

   (Self-counsel psychology series)
   Includes bibliographical references.
   ISBN 0-88908-975-2
1. Body image. 2. Women — Psychology.
3. Reducing — Social aspects. I. Title. II. Series.
BF697.5.B63C76   1991   155.6'33   C91-091652-7

Cover photo by Gary Ritchie Photography, New Westminster

Self-Counsel Press
(a division of)
International Self-Counsel Press Ltd.
Head and Editorial Office
1481 Charlotte Road
North Vancouver, British Columbia V7J 1H1
U.S. Address
1704 N. State Street
Bellingham, Washington 98225

CONTENTS

WORKSHEETS

ACKNOWLEDGMENTS

I would like to thank the many women who met me in my home, in their homes, in coffee shops, and in their professional offices and who so generously and often passionately shared their ideas. I appreciate the time the psychiatrists, psychologists, therapists, and family doctors spent with me. I would like to thank the many women who answered questionnaires, gave me interviews and who responded to this project with enthusiastic support, in particular: Sandy Friedman, Diana Douglas, Pat Touchie, Ruth Wilson, Arlene Trustham, Carrie Green, Gretchan Jordon Bastow, Jessie Swaile, Ella Little, Catherine Sperling, Madelein Hardin, and Pam Shantz.

INTRODUCTION

A perfect woman is tall, blond, and size ten. She makes money. She has two children and a husband. She is educated, accomplished, efficient, and organized.

Women told me that this was who they wanted to be, the woman they expected to be. Can't a woman be plump and short? Can't a woman be relaxed and satisfied? Can't a woman be single? Can't a woman be dark, swarthy, voluptuous, passionate, and fat?

"Of course, she can," the women told me. Intellectually, they were prepared to grant that women did not come in one mold and not everyone could be the "ideal" woman. White women, black women, Asian, Native, short, and poor women know this ideal is impractical, but still we want to be tall, blond, size ten, and rich.

Since only 8 percent of the population of women will naturally be size ten, what happens to the rest of us? Are we, therefore, not women? Or at least not women who are good enough? Are we failures?

That is ridiculous. The women I talked to agreed that it is ridiculous. We should be content with who we are, with how we look — unless of course plastic surgery, better clothes, a better face cream, better makeup, a new job, and daily dieting could make us more ideal.

How can we look at ourselves and appreciate what we see? How can we look at ourselves and feel joyous? How can we look at ourselves and feel grateful, accepting, sure that we have a unique, interesting, admirable combination of body and character that will accomplish great things and be happy? Can't we celebrate our bodies?

Many of us cannot.

I wrote a book for teenagers on the problems of anorexia nervosa and bulimia. While researching that book, I talked to 22 women who suffered from eating disorders. They told me how they viewed their bodies, what was important to them, how "looking good" was more important than jobs, family, accomplishments, relationships, more important than anything else in their lives. They told me how their bodies reflected what they felt. When they felt unhappy they saw themselves as fat and, therefore, repulsive. When they felt happy, they saw themselves as thin. They spent most of their day caring for their eating disorder, thinking about food, diets, fat, size, and the "perfect body." They had little time to enjoy life, friends, lovers, family, or job, and little time to learn anything new. They were intelligent, perceptive, warm, compassionate, and, to me, infinitely sad.

Most of us do not suffer from an eating disorder, but we probably have many of the same ideas on femininity, perfection, and body ideals. Many women do not like themselves. In our society, it seems "normal" to be dissatisfied. It upsets me to see women desperately trying to conform to an impossible ideal. Perfectly good, honest, courageous, loving women are trying to change themselves. It seems tragic, particularly for the young, to be pursuing an image of femininity that is born in media advertising. Why tall? Why blonde? Why size ten or even smaller? It makes me angry to see young women ignoring their choices. They should be reveling in the freedom that was won with such hard work by the generations before them; a freedom that can give them immeasurable choices of career and life-style. After a history of agitation for women's rights and two decades of active feminism, women are defining femininity in such a narrow manner they restrict their lives even more than in the past.

I was seething with questions:

> Are these women afraid of freedom?
>
> Do they have any positive role models to emulate?
>
> Do they see the restrictions of this "Barbie-doll" femininity?
>
> Why do they pursue such self-defeating ambitions?
>
> Where do women think they fit in society?
>
> What is their relationship to each other, to men?
>
> How do women feel about themselves?
>
> Do we want a certain body image to please ourselves, to please other women, or to please men?
>
> What difference does how we feel about ourselves make to us?
>
> What are women looking for?

The best way to find the answers was to ask women. I gathered a party of friends at my house, promising them dinner and asking if they would talk about body image. I couldn't control my friends so

I had no idea whether they would talk about body image or about the plight of women in South America, or the new whale pool at the Aquarium, or the current tax problem. I invited friends who were accomplished, financially independent, intelligent, and, of course, since they were my friends, warm, and compassionate. Eleven women came for dinner: an editor, two filmmakers, a therapist, a realtor, a publisher, a college teacher, the director of planning for a big hospital, the director of marketing for a publishing firm, and a sociologist/writer. They ate my lasagna, drank my wine, then seriously discussed women and body image. They were witty, persuasive, perceptive, and creative. They were less interested in giving me directions for the book than in exploring the subject of body image to satisfy themselves. These women put their considerable intelligence to the subject and gave me permission to use their comments.

Besides the concentrated efforts of my friends, I wanted opinions from women chosen at random, so I handed out questionnaires. My daughter gave questionnaires to her friends and acquaintances at her veterinary college. My youngest son gave questionnaires to his friends and acquaintances at his university on the opposite coast. I gave questionnaires to my neighbors, my bank manager, anyone who called to see me or phoned me. I sent out 50 questionnaires and had 31 returned. The comments were surprisingly frank.

Generally, women do not like their bodies. Much of the dissatisfaction seems to focus on size. Why do women want to be size ten? What do they do to try to achieve this? What is the pursuit of thinness doing to them? Why do women deliberately limit themselves by slavishly following an ideal body image? What are women looking for? I wanted to find the source of our dissatisfaction with our bodies.

When I tried to find out why women were pursuing an impossible body image, I thought back to my days in a small town, of the many women I had known and worked with in my life: the aggressive, independent public health nurses who disappeared for days in the bush by themselves, bringing vaccines and preventive medicine to rural areas, coming back to organize and administer their territories closer to home, getting together to work out problems, to commiserate, to laugh, and to support each other. I thought of the farm women who met to help each other at Women's Institute meetings; to provide a home for a burned-out family; to look after someone's child while the mother was in hospital, tend her garden, look after her animals. I remembered the women who talked to me about their problems, their hopes, their frustrations. I called all these women into my mind and then went out looking for more.

I spent hours in soul-searching conversation with women to research this book. I talked to nutritionists, nurses, doctors, psychiatrists, psychologists, teachers, students, dress shop owners, and therapists. I attended a support group for women with eating disorders. I read many, many books on the subject of women's ideas, ambitions, ideals, prejudices, and problems, trying to understand how we view our bodies and how that view affects our lives.

In the following chapters I bring you women's perspectives on themselves, so that you can better understand yourself and the social pressures that affect you, me, and all women. I want you to read, then lift your head and really look at the lives of other women, see the ways they are like you and the ways they are different.

This book outlines what our society considers ideal, and why we accept that ideal; how women were viewed in the past and how we came to accept controls on our lives. It shows the enormous burden of prejudice — blind, unfair, crippling prejudice — that most of us have accepted for years. It challenges the "health" myths that we learned very early in life. The first eight chapters help you consider what is happening to you and around you.

The final chapters outline some of the practical suggestions that many of the women I interviewed found helpful to create an atmosphere of acceptance. There is information on how these women deal with negative comments and how they maintain belief in themselves. You will also read about what others have done to make a difference in weight prejudice and what you can do to see yourself with faith, optimism, and even admiration.

Imagine that I have come to visit in your kitchen: you pour coffee and we sit and talk about body image. Let this book be a companion, a friend, a guide. We have a never-ending curiosity about ourselves. Why do we want to be thin? Why do we think that thin is magic? Why do we try so hard to be what we are not? Why can't we accept each other in a size and weight that is our own? This book can satisfy some of that curiosity, answer some of the questions, help you see what is happening around you and show you how to cope with it.

This book also tries to show how you can change your life, your family, and even society. It is not easy to change how you feel about yourself, but it is possible. In order to make changes, you need to understand what is happening to you, how you are trying to look after yourself in a society that ignores your needs. It takes reflection on your part to reach a new understanding. You must think about what you read, think about how your life is similar or different, think about what you want.

1

WHAT IS PERFECT?

Women are various and unique and yet share characteristics that make them alike. I know when I write about "women" and their body image that somewhere there is a woman who is different, whose body image is not the one common to most western women. One day she will stop me after a lecture and say, "You know, I've never felt like that. I've always liked myself." She is the woman the rest of us wish we were. She is the one we want our daughters to be, the one who is secure in her mind and in her body.

Most women don't have that security. Most women in this culture are dealing with pressures that make them unsure of their femininity and unaccepting of the way their bodies look. Joyce, a 35-year-old mother and homemaker said, "We are just overwhelmed with [the way we must look]. We are *required* to have perfect bodies. After being driven crazy with that, how can we possibly be satisfied with the way we are?"

a. THIN IS PERFECT

The perfect body is only one type, only one size. It is size ten. You may be accepted if you are smaller, but not if you are larger. To be feminine today is to be thin.

That is accepted as fact by most women. The women who answered my questionnaire sometimes wrote angry comments about the unfairness of this concept but no one questioned the reality of it. Thin is feminine and attractive. Like Joyce, they may resent the pressures on them to be that small size, but they accepted the fact that small is desirable.

Millions of women strive to be thin. Dieting is a $35-billion industry in North America. Intelligent, goal-setting, accomplished women work hard at trying to be thin. We wear our hair so that our faces will look thin. We buy clothes to show our bodies as thin (or thinner). We count calories to keep threatening fat away and believe that if we diet, we can be thinner. We *believe* those ads that say we can shrink to a model size. We spend hours exercising to get rid of cellulite or prevent it from forming. We try to keep our bodies looking eighteen years old and trim no matter what our age or what experiences our bodies have had. We do not expect our post-pregnancy bodies to be different from our pre-pregnancy bodies. We do not expect aging to affect us. We are, generally, intelligent women yet we strive for the impossible. We are like ravens, parrots, finches, eagles; all beautiful in our own way, yet all trying to be canaries.

b. THIN IS MAGIC

A woman often feels a small size is a magical size. At a small size all her dreams will come true. She will walk into a room and suddenly be admired, accepted. She will do all the things she has been planning to do — as soon as she loses weight. She will be accomplished, interesting, and sexually alluring. She will have power in society. She will be a woman like the women in the thousands of ads and movies and television programs she has seen since she was a child. When she is thin, all this will happen to her.

c. THIN IS ACCEPTABLE

She isn't always wrong. When a woman fits society's ideal she usually is admired and accepted. She is naturally the ideal size, she accepts it as normal for her and, because society reveres that weight, she finds more acceptance, more admiration than someone who does not fit that ideal. She can feel at home in her body and accept herself more easily than someone who is constantly fighting her body. From that acceptance comes feelings of self-esteem and a feeling that she has power to make her own way in the world.

If a woman is not naturally the "ideal" weight and has struggled to get there, she does not have her naturally-slim sister's feelings of acceptance and high self-esteem. Her acceptance of herself is based on her weight and will disappear as her weight returns. She wastes time and energy maintaining her weight and, unlike the woman who is naturally thin, does not feel the sense of integration or acceptance. The magical changes may not happen for her, or may happen for her only in the week she feels thin.

d. WHY WOMEN WANT TO BE PERFECT: BODY IMAGE AND THE MEDIA

When we look around us in the media and in our social world and discover the ideal North American woman, we find that she does not occupy much space. She is pencil-thin, trim, and can slide through the established social world like a shadow. She is attractive, decorative, accomplished, intelligent, and she is small enough to be overlooked and ignored.

She does not have the round hips and tummy of a mature woman. The "ideal" North American woman has small breasts, no hips, and no tummy. She generally looks like a pre-pubescent girl or boy. Models with this look are hard to find among "grown-ups" so some magazines use very young girls to model women's clothes. The "ideal" North American woman then, is often not a woman at all.

The "ideal" North American woman does not have any hair on her body other than the hair on her head. Again, like a pre-pubescent girl or boy she has no hair on her legs, under her arms, or in her pubic area. She does not have the sexual characteristics of a flesh and blood woman.

We are growing up with this androgynous ideal dictated to us through the media by the fashion and fitness industry. Women strive to change themselves to approximate as closely as possible this socially acceptable look. When most women with normal female development deposit fat on their hips and tummies, grow hair in appropriate places and get larger, they don't feel as though they are getting more feminine — they feel they are getting ugly, unacceptable, out of control, and further away from their tiny, thin goal.

Presently, eight percent of our female population is naturally the ideal size. The next generation will have an even smaller percentage of the population naturally at that size. Our infant and childhood nutrition is encouraging a bigger generation. So while the media ideal female is getting smaller, the average North American woman is getting larger. This dichotomy is creating more and more women who feel unacceptable and unattractive.

e. THE MEDIA MYTH IN THE MIND

The difference between what we think we *should* be and what we think we *are* creates confusion and pain in the minds of many women. The image the mirror sends to us is not the ideal image society tells us every woman should be. The image in the mirror is real, but not what most women want. Many women cannot accept the evidence of their eyes and either change themselves through constant dieting, or change their mental concept of their bodies, or change a little of both so that they can live in peace with themselves.

Some believe they have an inner core which remains admirable and acceptable and which is unrelated to their physical body. They divorce their minds from their bodies and reject their physical appearance. Many women have difficulty knowing what size they are because their mental body image is so very different from their physical body. Many women — perfectly normal women in other respects — talk about their bodies as if they didn't belong to them, or as if their bodies were only with them temporarily and were going to be traded in for a better model tomorrow or next week. These women feel as if their minds and their bodies are in conflict. Some deal with this by never really seeing below their necks. They comb their hair and apply makeup to their faces but never acknowledge the rest of their bodies.

Some women do not divorce themselves entirely from their bodies, but concentrate on rejecting certain parts.

"I hate my hips."

"If I could just do something about my ankles."

"My nose is so big; it's ugly."

In their minds they isolate those parts, labelling them as either temporary or non-existent. Such acrobatics of the brain take energy. At some level these women are not satisfied with the way they are coping.

f. THE EFFECTS OF THE PERFECT BODY MYTH

When women do not accept their own bodies, when they hate their size and hate their weight, they have trouble believing that other people can accept them. They are unsure of their place in society, unsure of their welcome. They are like apologetic water reeds bending in the wind of social opinion, ready to drift to another position, never sure they belong in this space, never rooted securely. This affects their lives profoundly as individuals, friends, mothers, wives, and, especially, as lovers. The effects of a narrow feminine ideal are crippling.

To find out how committed you are to the impossible body image, fill out Worksheet #1.

g. WILL THIS MYTH BE WITH US FOREVER?

Women's preoccupation with weight, with "looking good," with becoming an impossible size ten, has pervaded our society because we have a diet-industry-driven media bias, because our parents and our teenaged peers interpret that bias to us as a reality, and because we accept that bias as fact. It isn't fair, and we shouldn't put up with it.

But it doesn't have to be with us forever. We can make changes. We can reassess our lives and find a comfortable body image that allows us freedom from diets and body sculpting, that stimulates social acceptance. We have a wide variety of sizes and weights in our culture, and we need, as individual women, and as a society, to accept that.

WORKSHEET #1
ASSESSING YOUR COMMITMENT TO AN IMPOSSIBLE BODY IMAGE

	YES	NO
1. Do you think thin women are generally more competent than overweight women?	❏	❏
2. Do you think that thin women are generally more able to feel sexual pleasure and excitement than overweight women?	❏	❏
3. Are most of the women you admire slim?	❏	❏
4. Do you want to be thinner?	❏	❏
5. Do you wish parts of your body would disappear?	❏	❏
6. Do you think you would have more choice of sexual partners if you were thinner?	❏	❏
7. Do you think that job opportunities would be greater if you were thinner?	❏	❏
8. Do you put off activities or beginning relationships until the time when you will be thinner?	❏	❏
9. Do you think overweight people do not deserve a job promotion, a sexual partner, admiration, or respect?	❏	❏
10. Do you think most women can and should be slim?	❏	❏
11. Do you think that most women do not try hard enough to be slim?	❏	❏
12. Do you consider yourself "bad" when you eat certain foods and "good" when you restrict your eating?	❏	❏
13. Do you consider yourself overweight?	❏	❏

If you answered yes more than once to questions 1 through 8, you have been persuaded, like millions of other women, that the body you have is not good enough and that another, thinner one would magically create a world of success and opportunity for you.

If you answered yes to any of questions 9 through 12, you have absorbed the message "thin is good; fat is bad" that makes size and weight a moral issue in our culture. Consider what such a prejudiced attitude does to your life, the lives of your sons and daughters, your neighbors and friends. Consider the anxiety that is created by this moral judgment, the criticism, the pressure on self-esteem that comes from believing in the good or bad of a particular size and weight.

If you answered yes to question 13, as most women do, you think you are not good enough as you are. Are you ever going to be "good enough"? Perhaps, instead of changing your weight you can work on changing your attitude to your body.

2

HOW BODY IMAGE MYTHS INFLUENCE US

a. THE TEEN YEARS

Looking back at my teenaged years, I remember the humiliating time when my body was never good enough. Marilyn Monroe had breasts; Marion Crook did not. Her knees were dimpled; mine were bony. It wasn't much help to realize that most teens feel this way.

Most teens still believe that they are the only ones who don't fit, who have a dumpy body, who are awkward, ugly, fat. If they are part of a social group that emphasizes sports or theater or just one that does not overemphasize "looking good," such humiliation is only an occasional burden. Those in a loving, supportive, and encouraging family have help to cushion social humiliations. They are at least accepted at home.

But many teens live in families who are controlling and critical. They socialize with other teens who think "looking good" is the only worthwhile goal and who practice small cruelties on teens who do not measure up to their standards.

Some teachers make belittling remarks in class. Others, in an effort to help, suggest weight reduction, ballet, or modeling classes. In both cases, the teacher passes a judgment that the teenager understands too well — she isn't good enough as she is.

Such experiences drive some teens to a kind of despair about their bodies. They believe family members and schoolmates who say they are too fat to be loved, too ugly to be wanted, too fat to be successful.

If our body image is formed in the teen years, as some theorists believe, it is no wonder that so many women have a poor one. We add fat to our bodies in preparation for menstruation but the very fat that declares us to be women is considered by society to be unfeminine. We then frantically try to take off the fat so we look like pre-pubescent girls. It's as confusing as the virgin mother concept.

Teenaged years should be the time we learn about relationships. It should be the time we learn to understand depth of character, ambitions, emotions. When teens spend most of their time, money, and energy on the body beautiful, relationships tend to center around the body beautiful as well. It is easy to become enmeshed in superficial and shallow pursuits, to miss opportunities to understand ourselves and the people around us. When the teen years are spent "looking good," so many of us miss the chance to develop the tools we need to maintain relationships and to judge character.

The pursuit of thinness creates a life that excludes other more interesting aspects of living: developing skills and hobbies, developing character and personality, and finding and keeping friends.

Adults who spent their teen years obsessed with their bodies may have trouble judging themselves realistically. They may have missed lying back on the grass, gazing up at the clouds wondering who they were, what they believed in, what mattered in the world to them, where they fit in it. And they may be without a dependable, positive body image. Most young women, after all, will never be size ten, so they pass through those years of constant striving to find they are ashamed of their body. They resent it. They want a different one, a smaller one, a thinner one. No wonder their self-esteem is low.

b. INSECURITY AND LACK OF SELF-ESTEEM

If we consider our body to be "normal" and attractive, we usually have the confidence that we will "look good" or, at least, "look normal" in most social situations. Much space in women's magazines is devoted to how to create the right "image" for working, for parties, for sexual adventures. Feeling socially acceptable gives us confidence.

When a woman is convinced that her body is repulsive, abnormal, fat, she may never feel socially acceptable. She may avoid situations where she will be noticed. That makes any job that puts her in front of people hard for her to even consider. From her low self-esteem comes the feeling that people are criticizing her, talking about her, putting her down. She may be so reluctant to meet new people that she puts up with a dentist or doctor she does not like because she does not want to risk the judgment of a new one or puts up with a job she hates because she is afraid to move.

When a woman is convinced that she has a "sub-standard" body, she often sees herself as not deserving acceptance. "No wonder no one wants me around; I'm too fat." In that state of mind, her low self-esteem blocks her involvement in society and her personal development.

But her conviction that she is not acceptable is not based on whether or not she is actually accepted or on her real appearance. Once she believes she is unacceptable she stops trying. She pulls back from social activities — her daughter's skating club, a night school course, the local historical society. She feels she does not deserve to be with others. Since the ideal weight is so low and most women's weight falls outside the ideal, many women in our society feel undeserving.

c. RELATIONSHIPS

1. Parents

Some women have relationships that reinforce their feelings of being undeserving. They may have a complaining parent who constantly criticizes them. Often, with the intention of "helping" the daughter, a parent will make suggestions, give advice, and offer solutions to problems, making it clear that the daughter is incompetent and unacceptable as she is. A friend of mine said, "I love my body; my husband loves my body. So should I *care* what my mother thinks?" She does, of course, but maintains her positive attitude in spite of her mother.

2. Husbands and lovers

Many women live with a husband or partner who constantly criticizes. Some partners want a size ten woman on their arm so that they will look successful. Some demand the impossible size ten so the woman is always failing. Knowing that size ten is impossible and still demanding it as a condition of love puts the husband or partner in a position of perpetual power. When the woman can never achieve that "reasonable" goal, she doesn't feel equal to him. Holding the balance of power is exactly what he wants.

3. Other women

There are other aspects of control and social power that seem to blossom in weight issues. Some women want to be "better than" other women. They are anxious that other women look worse than they do, that other women weigh more, have "trouble" with their weight. They feel better about themselves if they think other women look worse. They are committed to the principle that "looking good" is the most important accomplishment of their lives. They can be unkind, sarcastic, even cruel (and silly, I might add) without seeing themselves that way.

A woman who is "overweight" and who accepts herself anyway may be grudged her happiness by one of these envious overly-competitive women. "If she's fat, she *shouldn't* be happy." Others might feel that such an woman should be dieting and suffering. It is difficult to ignore that kind of envy.

d. SEXUALITY

Through our teen years, through the relationships with our parents and then our partners and friends, we develop a sense of who we are. Included in this self-definition is our concept of our feminine body. Inherent in this sense of being feminine is our understanding, acceptance, and use of our sexuality.

Anne said, "But we are so concerned about our body image because we are concerned about sex. I mean the reason we have to have this beautiful body is so that some man will have sex with us. Really. And want to marry us and have kids."

Susan could not leave that statement unchallenged. "But sexual attraction is different for different people. I don't think sexuality has anything to do with what we define as sexually attractive. I think it's a total opposite. I think walking down the street and wanting to have sex with somebody is an incredibly hostile and objectifying act."

Me: What about evaluation: "This one is attractive. That one doesn't attract?"

Anne: That's not objectifying.

Me: I suppose it's just a dressed up version of objectifying, isn't it?

Susan: Sure it is.

Women usually do not think only a man's body is sexually attractive. We look at a package — personality, smile, smell, attitudes, voice. But it seems that more and more young women particularly are stressing the appearance of a man's body, a stereotyped body, as more important than anything else. Yet we know that it is not just the response to a person's appearance that constitutes sexual attractiveness. Nor is it a response to just one body type. Some people are far more attracted to smells than appearance. Some are attracted to a warm smile, a sense of humor, affectionate touching.

To define sexual attractiveness only as appearance — a male "hunk" or a thin woman — is ludicrous. Yet millions of women grow up believing that sexual attractiveness is limited to a size ten body. It may take years, perhaps twenty years, before they realize that life is a good deal richer and more varied than the movies led them to believe and that sexual attractiveness is an individual response.

So we live for years with a sense of inadequacy because we do not fit what we think is sexually attractive. And all that time we ignore or underrate the sexually attractive qualities that come with our unique size, shape, and personality. We underrate the attractiveness of a confident, intriguing personality. We underrate the sexual attractiveness of round feminine curves. We underrate the positive qualities of a healthy, functioning body.

Many women feel their bodies are a disadvantage to their sex life. Since bodies are the medium through which we enjoy sex, this conviction must seriously affect spontaneity and sensual pleasure. If a woman divorces her mind from her body or hates the look of her body, she is seriously handicapped in the open, joyous, and mutually satisfying pleasures of sexual activity. If she does not like the medium she is using, how can she enjoy what she is doing? When a women feels uncomfortable in sexual situations because she dislikes her body, this compounds her feeling of being left out of the feminine world. What should be profoundly satisfying and enriching becomes another arena of failure.

e. PHYSICAL AND VERBAL ABUSE

Envision what happens to a young woman who is 5'4" (163 cm) and 152 pounds (70 kg). She is, by Metropolitan Life and by U.S. National Research Council 1989 standards, overweight but she accepts herself as a beautiful, big woman who has a lot to be proud of. She approaches life as a confident person. She is unwilling to accept poor treatment and definitely will not accept abuse. Why should she?

Contrast her with another young woman of the same height and weight. She takes the social attitude to weight, internalizes it, and makes it part of her personal beliefs. She may be healthy and beautiful, but, if she believes she is abnormal, she will probably start the self-defeating and humiliating yo-yo life of dieting. If she feels that she is unappealing and does not deserve to be accepted by society, she may accept poor treatment from others, perhaps even abuse.

Many women accept verbal abuse from others — "Don't you think you should lose a few pounds?" (translation "You are not good enough as you are") — so that it has become common practice to criticize size and weight. Often, these women also belittle themselves as "weak," "fat," and "undisciplined."

f. SEXUAL ABUSE

Many women have experienced sexual abuse, either once or repeatedly. We may have dealt with the effect on our lives or we may have ignored what happened, putting it behind us and getting on with living. But such blows to our self-esteem, to our integrity, to our feelings of safety and security still influence how we feel about ourselves.

That influence can be seen in women with eating disorders who are obsessively committed to the socially accepted perfect size. "Looking good" is all important to them. Recent statistics show that 66 percent of women with eating disorders were sexually abused. Sexual abuse didn't cause eating disorders but it may have been the root cause in these women's low self-esteem.

Sexual abuse is also likely to have had an effect on women whose relationship with food and diets is not as extreme as eating disorders. Think about how that abuse might influence body image. The way they dress for instance. Do they try to hide their bodies in clothes or in fat? Do they treat their bodies as if they were only machines that carry their brains, or as if they were only sex objects?

The problems of the effects of sexual abuse can better be dealt with by therapists than in this book but the influence of such abuse should be recognized here. It is, no doubt, crucial to some women's concept of their body image. It may be behind their understanding of how they use their body and how they think others see it.

g. WHO BENEFITS FROM WOMEN'S INSECURITIES?

It is not hard to see that some segments of society benefit when women are preoccupied with weight and physical appearance. The billion-dollar-per-year diet and beauty industry feeds upon the constant insecurity of so much of the female population. Maintaining this industry requires maintaining the insecurity.

Women who are preoccupied with their physical appearance are distracted from the job market, from ambitions, and from positions that require energy and time. The lack of self-esteem that arises from pursuit of an impossible goal prevents women from grasping opportunities and competing with men. Some men find this sad and feel cheated of women's contributions. Some men are relieved that they have less competition in the job market.

Women who depend on others for a sense of worth tend to be dependent on men's acceptance and on men for their security. This is not seen as a positive attribute by many men, but is seen as positive by some.

Thin women in a business world may appear easier to control and easier to ignore. Susan, my friend and a therapist, said, "The women who are the least threatening to some men are the women who are not there; and the way to be not there is to look like a pencil."

Whatever the underlying social reasons for demanding an impossible body size, women are aware of the pressures on them to be thin. Many women are angry that their voluptuous size fourteen body is often seen as "abnormal." Yet, these same women may try to reduce that size fourteen to a size ten and spend years dieting.

We do not usually recognize these pressures as myths, oppressive and restricting. We accept such pressures as real and respond by trying to force our bodies into a socially acceptable size and shape. We want our bodies to be considered feminine and attractive. We need to start seeing such pressures as oppressive fairy tales, the myths of our time.

3

WHY WE ACCEPT THE BODY IMAGE MYTH

It is obvious that some people in society see benefits to a restrained role for women, but why would women want it? With our wonderful tools of energy and intelligence, why do we, as a group, accept such slavish restrictions?

Historically, women conformed to the fashion-binding dictates slowly, over years, emulating what seem to be harmless models, accepting unsupported "medical" or "health" advice, uncritically cooperating with others, fitting into society.

Women today may feel a great responsibility to be not only acceptable but superb, to be better than our mothers, to change, to lead the way for a generation of competent, empowered women. We feel a strong drive to be successful. Our problem lies in our definition of success. Success is not size ten.

a. LOW SELF-ESTEEM

Many women depend on others for their self-acceptance. Many women only accept themselves if their husbands accept them or their mothers accept them. Some women only accept themselves and feel confident about themselves if husband, mother, boss, children, teachers, bus driver — everyone in their lives — accepts them at all times. Such external control of their self-esteem is doomed to failure. It is like having the thermostat of your self-esteem furnace constantly turned up and down by family members, even visitors.

Jeanne, 66, grey-haired, energetic, a writer and social worker, was a guest at my body-image dinner. She said, "Whether we dress for women or for men, the issue here is that we look outside ourselves for a definition of how we should be, and try to live up to it."

Teresa: "Is that a problem? I mean, who doesn't?"

Jeanne: "The problem is that we lose our sense of self."

b. FAMILY PRESSURES

We are taught from the time we are little that there is an ideal body size and appearance. The media preaches a gospel of tall, blond, and size ten, in advertisements, entertainments, videos, and book covers. Such a credo is interpreted and intensified by a girl's family where parents urge daughters to dress well, to stay slim, and to make themselves attractive. Parents look at the weight prejudice around them and want their daughters to escape the censure of others, so they urge them to conform. Most parents accept the social axiom that life will be easier if women are slim. Some parents, of course, happily ignore the prejudice and urge their daughters to be competent, skillful, productive, and accepting of themselves as they are. But most parents are anxious that their daughters have all the advantages they can get for them, including a slim body.

c. FEAR OF CHOICE

Opportunities for women are greater today than at almost any other time in history. The choice of if and when to have children and the opening up of careers previously closed to women free women to consider many possibilities. Such choices may be frightening to women not conditioned or coached on how to choose. Choice may make a restrictive, limited life look "safe." Because they are frightened and have little guidance, some women bolt for what looks safe: size ten, fragile, and "feminine."

Many girls see opportunities and independence as unfeminine. They believe that a feminine woman needs protection, and if she needs protection, a man will protect her. They believe this in spite of the divorce rate, in spite of the single mothers abandoned by their mates, in spite of all the evidence around them to the contrary. They do not measure the cost of such a childlike existence. Women are conditioned to abdicate their responsibility for themselves. It may take years for them to realize that they are responsible, that they must make their own place in society. And they may never develop the confidence to do this.

d. LACK OF ROLE MODELS

We do not find role models abounding in a wide variety of weights. Public figures try to be slim. Very few public women accept their large bodies — Rita MacNeil is one of the wonderful exceptions. Most large women tell us that their big bodies are evidence of their personal failure. It is difficult to consider a womanly figure with fat deposits on tummy and hips as normal when so few women of intellect and accomplishments accept themselves that way.

e. FEAR OF SEXUALITY

In spite of our "free and accepting" social mores on sexual behavior, many women do not accept their own sexual feelings. The less they feel sexually, the more comfortable they are with their bodies. On the other hand, some women see themselves as only sexual objects. They think that everyone, male or female, is looking for opportunities to violate them. Those women are caught between trying to look as much like a sex object as they can in order to appear socially acceptable, while trying not to attract sexual attention. They are confused about their own sexuality, accept an inaccurate social definition of sexual attractiveness, and try to deny parts of their nature.

Such confusion and unsolved conflict about sexuality leads women into uncertainty about their body image and problems with their self-esteem. Sexuality is definitely part of our body image, definitely part of the image we let others see, definitely one source of our concept of our body. We need to consider our sexuality as good, healthy, normal, wonderful, and an integral part of ourselves.

When we consider the bruising so many women receive early in life to their concept of themselves as sexual people, we can understand how difficult it is for some women to accept themselves as sexual. It seems simpler to deny our wide and varied sexuality and define sexual attraction in terms of the perfect size ten.

f. LACK OF ALTERNATIVES

Today we are so ensnared in the body image trap that alternatives to the pursuit of thinness are not obvious to us. We do not see acceptance of a large size as a reasonable alternative. Culturally, we attribute to big women characteristics of carelessness, weakness, poor health, lack of accomplishment, sexual isolation, and laziness, whether or not they fit. Thanks to media conditioning, we belittle large women in spite of the fact that most of us know large women who do not fit the stereotype, and in spite of the fact that we may be large ourselves.

g. CONFORMING IN ORDER TO BELONG

The ideal woman, the woman our society admires, has changed over many centuries, within many cultures. She may be tall and black in Fiji, short and dark in Italy, blond in Norway. She may have been thin with a protruding belly in fifteenth century England; fair and plump during the Renaissance in Italy; big-breasted and narrow-waisted in the 1950s in North America; and small-breasted, thin, and androgynous today. She has moved though the centuries formed by public opinion: pulled in here and pushed out there; restricted by high heels, corsets, and tight bands; encouraged to eat in one country and starved in another.

At any time in most cultures, there is tremendous pressure on men and women to conform in order to belong. Humans are social animals; we have a strong need to belong to a group. We intrinsically understand, even as young children, that it is much easier to survive within the group than outside it. Even rebels seek like-minded people to form a group. We find acceptance within a group, and even in our North American culture, which presently stresses independence and individualism, we have overwhelmingly strong instincts to form groups. Most people have a work group, a social group, a religious group. Some have an encounter group, a bowling group, a study group. Finding a social group that accepts you as you are is a strong, normal human drive.

A social group distinguishes itself with beliefs, values, and rules of dress and behavior. While a woman may gravitate to a group that holds values she personally holds, it is also likely that her values are shaped by the social conditioning that comes from the rules, codes, and values important to that group.

There are great rewards for conforming to the rules of the group: psychological or emotional benefits such as acceptance, admiration, status, and support as well as physical benefits such as money, opportunities, comfort, position, marriage, and sexual opportunities. It is both emotionally satisfying and physically rewarding to conform to the rules of the social group.

h. SOCIAL PRESSURES TO CONFORM

Our ideal image comes from the needs of our social group. What is valued in one group, for instance wealth, becomes a value that influences how we see ourselves.

If our group values fertility (suppose our small tribe is threatened with extinction) then pregnancy is welcomed and any woman capable of becoming pregnant is valued. A pregnant woman becomes the ideal woman, and through association of ideas, so does any woman with large breasts and a protruding abdomen who resembles a pregnant woman. In this society, a women who by choice remains a virgin or who physically resembles a non-child-bearing adolescent may not be socially accepted. There is a strong social pressure on her to produce children so that the group will survive.

In our western culture, our economy needs wealth, so we value wealth and look for it in the ideal woman. A woman with money can afford expensive haircuts, facials, and fitness memberships that make her look young and thin. She can get her tan in the Bahamas in January (when the rest of us are pale) to represent the wealth that her group admires. Those who can't afford the Bahamian tan try to look as though they can, with sessions at tanning salons or by using tanning pills and creams.

The thin, tall, blond, fit, beautiful, rich woman satisfies the economic need of our culture to consume products. She consumes thousands of dollars of products to look like that and her imitators consume millions more in repeated, failed attempts to look like her. The economy is married to the sale of products, and the constant barrage of media inducements and media "truths" perpetuates the myth of the "ideal" woman.

Thinness embodies our social value of wealth. Because we value wealth, we also value thinness. In days gone by, when most of the population did not have enough to eat, fat was a status symbol, a symbol of wealth. You (or your husband) could provide enough to eat and more. Today, in western society, when most people can feed themselves adequately, fat does not suggest wealth. Today, thinness suggests wealth, since it costs money to join fitness clubs or go to health spas to attain the expensive ideal look.

The value placed on looking good in our society outweighs considerations of character, personality, productivity, and social contributions. This value is not a product of our need for attracting a mate and reproducing the species. It is a product of our economic market.

We live in a world that, in many different ways, pressures us to adapt, conform, and obey social rules. We are conditioned since childhood to drop our litter in containers, wait in lines at the bank, stand up when we hear the national anthem, leave the building when a fire bell rings. We conform also to the way our social group behaves, to the general dress code, the way we answer the telephone. We even tend to socialize in the same way as our friends, go to bingo, go to the opera, shop, watch the hockey games.

We have a strong need to belong, so it is not surprising that we would try to look like our social group, like the social ideal. We are urged by society to strive for the ideal size ten and we see social rewards for achieving that ideal. There are even social rewards for *trying* to achieve that ideal. Women on diets are often considered to be disciplined, responsible, and womanly.

We accept the body image myth because we want to belong and because we are conditioned, to believe what we know is unreasonable. It takes an enormous amount of creative energy and determination to break free of such a social group.

But we can break free. We can make changes. When we understand the economic, social, and personal pressures on us to conform, we can throw off those pressures. There are ripples of discontent across the continent. Women are beginning to speak out against size and weight prejudice. They are beginning to see how crippling such prejudice and pressures are to them.

Enough women need to be committed to changing the present body image ideal to a new one that is tolerant of varied size and weight. We must form a new social group whose rules and codes for a body image ideal allow all women to be beautiful in their own way.

4

CREATING THE IDEAL: PAST AND PRESENT

Throughout history women have tried to emulate ideals in order to gain social acceptance and social admiration.

a. THE IDEAL WOMAN IN EARLY HISTORY

1. Early cultures

Preserving the tribe had a high value in the early days of humanity. Clothing protected the genitals not out of modesty but out of the need to protect what kept the race from dying out. And even in those early days, some of the clothing placed over and around men and women's sexual parts were worn to attract attention to those parts, ensuring that procreation got encouragement. Social rules were the tribe's effort to keep the group together. Conformity to those rules meant a greater chance of survival.

Even today, how people look and what they wear shows their station within a society and what is important to that society. Conformity also gives power to the individual. The person is no longer alone; she is part of a bigger group who look similar to her.

In 2600 B.C. in Mesopotamia, the Sumerians had a culture of freedom. The Laws of Hammurabi, which came later, reflected the freedom and rational order in this society. Women were strong and equal in relationship to men. Divorce was easy and child support and alimony were available. Women worked and had paid sick leave and menstrual leave. Women went into business, although divorced women forfeited their alimony and child support when they did. Anyone who thinks our present preoccupation with size ten is a result of a society that gives choices to women should study the Sumerians.

Clothing was loose and flowing. Probably body size was unimportant since it could get bigger and smaller under such clothing without attracting much notice. Instead, hair styles were elaborate.

The "ideal" woman probably took time to arrange her hair, manicure her nails, and make up her face.

In Egypt in 1400 B.C., society seems to have placed importance on grooming. Men and women combed their hair, bathed, and applied perfumed oils often. Women had some freedom and choice, at least in the upper strata of society. Divorce was easy in Egypt and women held property. Drawings and paintings from Egypt at this time show everyone, men and women, slim with wide shoulders and narrow hips. We can only speculate on how this affected the social life of this time, but it is unlikely that everyone fit this idealized picture. Only foreigners are portrayed as fat.

2.   The Middle Ages: England and Europe

In the Middle Ages, appearance reflected social status. Servants did not emulate their "betters"; they dressed as servants. Nobility dressed distinctively and laws protected the difference. In 1362, an English statute restricted carters, ploughmen, oxherds, cowherds, swineherds, shepherds, and dairymen to buying undyed cloth or russet cloth at one shilling per yard. Their clothing had to be made from this material, making it easy to distinguish among the classes of society.

Women used their bodies to show religious piety. Fasting was practiced for religious reasons in the Middle Ages although it was not a social standard. Historically, there is a religious significance to fasting girls. What is considered anorexic today was considered saintly. A girl defying the hunger of the flesh must be embracing the spirit of God. Fasting gave the girl some status as a saint, and some claim to nobility in an age when women had few areas open to them in which to succeed. Under semi-starvation conditions, many fasting people had hallucinations, "visions," which added to their aura of piety.

An anorexic, "pious" girl was socially admired in a culture where superstition and religion were oppressive and pervasive.

Many religions bound fasting to holiness, and even today a girl who is physically weak from self-imposed starvation evokes a kind of awe and admiration from others who view her as a "spiritually" strong individual and not one who is suffering emotionally.

In spite of the social attention such girls gained, anorexia, although held up as an ideal in some cultures, was not widely copied. Even dieting was not common.

3. The first diet

In 1558, an Italian, Luigi Coronaro, advocated a sparse diet that had changed him from a sick, overweight man to an energetic, thin one. His persuasive writings convinced many. Coronaro's diet is one of the first recorded instances of the magical promises of the diet. The idea of dieting to change your life, dieting to live forever, captured many converts to the cause of dieting.

For centuries people have labelled the reasons for obesity to indicate their search for some magical cause and solution to the problem. Overweight has been attributed to dyspepsia (malfunctioning digestion), nervous exhaustion, virtue or lack of virtue, endocrine gland disorder, too many calories, and lack of exercise. In efforts to make life simple, overweight people have tried fantastic "cures": opium, vomiting, bitters, iron waters, mercurial medicines, and laxatives. Today, almost 450 years later, diets still capture the dreams of the people.

4. The seventeenth century

In seventeenth century England, servants were no longer restricted by law to specific clothing. When they could, they copied their masters' and mistresses' fashions, and wore their employers' cast-off clothing. Fashion and the ideas around fashion began to move out from the nobility into a wider social group. All levels of society began to believe in the possibility of change.

Sexual attractiveness at this time depended more on overall appearance than on how much one weighed. Both men and women used clothing to create an image that was admired. Padding and lacing could convert almost any figure into an "ideal" one.

Dieting in the seventeenth century was the practice of middle-aged men who lived "well," the corpulent example of prosperity. Fat people were accepted since only the rich could afford enough food to become fat. Dieting became a health activity recommended for obese aristocrats.

b. THE EIGHTEENTH CENTURY

1. Pre-revolution France

In Europe and its colonies, the eighteenth century was an era dominated by French fashion with richly decorated elaborate designs. Everything, including furniture and buildings, was elaborately curled or adorned with flowers, angels, ruffles, and lace.

The Court of Versailles influenced the western world's concept of what was "ideal." Women were elaborately and expensively dressed and coiffed, they had pink and white complexions, and they were slightly plump. Breasts were considered fashionable and so were revealed with deep, wide necklines. Women were not limited to one size at this time, but were judged by the way they were clothed.

Women's fashions were not meant to be functional, only to be admired. Long trains and yards of heavy material made walking difficult. Shoes were made for display, not for function.

The ideal was a result of many complex pressures from society. After the economic problems that followed France's war with Spain, the French government stimulated the domestic silk industry by encouraging a fashion of women's dresses with such wide skirts that they required many yards of silk. It also became the fashion for women to wear a different dress to each ball, increasing the profits to the merchants.

Fashionable skirts were so wide that it was sometimes difficult for women to move through doors, sit down, or walk in the streets. Such elaborate fashions, created to satisfy the economic needs of the silk traders, imprisoned women in a useless, unproductive "ideal." Such fashions sometimes killed them: if a woman's gown caught fire, she would be dead before she could get out of it; if she fell from a boat, her heavy skirts would drag her under.

2. Equality

The French Revolution in 1789 quickly and dramatically changed the ideal in France and, because France was the leader of fashion, in all Europe. Elaborately dressed women were seen as traitors to the New Regime. Simplicity became desirable. The social order was turned upside down and men and women struggled to establish an ideal that reflected the egalitarian mood of the times. The threat of the guillotine was an incentive to a quick fashion change.

In America, the spirit of independence required similar restraint in dress and the ideal women looked more like the working class woman. But in England the working class woman struggled to be like and look like the nobility.

c. THE NINETEENTH CENTURY

In nineteenth century America, society became more established, and while Americans picked up fashions from Europe, they also

established a fashion of their own. While women were not equal —
they did not have the right to vote — they had some degree of
personal freedom. Women could plan their families, abortion was
common, and women were becoming more vocal and more obviously interested in examining their lives.

1. The healthy ideal

In 1830, Dioclesian Lewis established a new vision of health. He
founded the New Gymnastics: exercise in conjunction with a simple
life of fresh air, long walks, and two simple meals a day. He lectured
and wrote books, converting many to the virtues of a healthy life. He
admired not thinness alone, but health and vigor.

In 1834 in New England, the Reverend Sylvester Graham advocated a simple diet of three meals a day consisting of home-baked
bread, vegetables, fruit, and milk, with no snacks, condiments, coffee, tea, or ale, and, an almost revolutionary idea for the time, no
beef. He was interested in social reform and thought that he could
achieve it through diet. He thought that by establishing a frugal,
simple, and wholesome diet at home, mothers could curb the ex-
cesses of their families. Diet was going to introduce a new morality.

This simple diet was heavily criticized by many, but taken up by
those who saw it as a way to become healthy by losing weight. Dr.
Graham's diet was one of the first reducing diets in America. The
dieters worked toward a natural, individual weight that represented
individual health, a concept that this generation seems to have lost.

2. The American woman's preoccupation with weight

In spite of the health-oriented concept that each person is unique and
is healthy at a different weight, the playbills, fashion plates, and
poems of the time all held thinness to be admirable.

In the 1850s, Reverend David Macrae from Scotland was struck
by the American woman's pursuit of thinness. He commented that
most women knew their weight and would talk about it often.

Forerunners to the weight clinic, water baths and spas developed in the 1840s. Usually run by women, these spas took women
in for a rest cure and treated them with water immersions, vegetarian
diets, and water to drink — an unusual beverage for that era. Weight
loss was the aim of the cure. Abortions were sometimes the effect of
the water treatment and, no doubt, the goal of some of the clients.

In the latter part of the century, men wore less form-fitting clothes and could put on weight without it being obvious. A woman's clothes still revealed her figure.

After the American Civil War, "exhaustion" was a common ailment. If a person was fat, he or she complained of exhaustion and looked for a physical cure. It related to the "dyspepsia" of the past and the "overweight" of the future. Although largely an emotional problem, exhaustion was often labelled neurasthenia and treated as a physical complaint with diet and rest. Just as today, the dissatisfactions of a woman's life were focused on her weight, and weight loss became the answer to all problems.

d. THE EARLY TWENTIETH CENTURY

1. The war on fat

The 1880s saw the birth of the science of home economics giving housewives status. The housewife became a "manager" with "science" behind her. As a scientist, she became determined to measure, predict, and control everything in her domestic world, including fat.

By 1910, home economists had declared war on fat. Fat was subjected to scientific analysis, its properties discussed and speculated upon. Fat was the perfect subject for fanatical zealots, disgruntled physicians, keen home economists, and well-intentioned mothers because it could be subjected to any kind of "cure." Once the public knew that fat was bad, they would try almost anything to get rid of it.

2. The tyranny of height/weight charts

By the late nineteenth century, many life insurance studies indicated that overweight men died earlier than men who were not overweight. Their studies were suspect but unchallenged. In order to sell insurance, they needed to convince the buyer that he was vulnerable to death. The narrower the ideal weight, the more vulnerable the majority of the population appeared at an earlier age. Their studies did not accept average weight as a natural weight. Instead, they picked a low-weight ideal, wrongly implying that a low weight would prevent death. Anything more than their "ideal" was considered overweight. They picked out these studies on men and applied them to women, creating an amazing chart of inaccurate, inapplicable, impractical, and dangerously misleading information that influenced the thinking of the public for decades.

3.   Standard sizes and skimpy styles

Before 1919, women either made their own clothes or had their clothes made to fit. Clothes for fat women were as chic and interesting as clothes for thin women. But in 1919, ready-made clothes with their limiting standard sizes appeared. After the introduction of standard sizes, those who did not fit the sizes were made to feel sub-standard, abnormal. Non-fashionable bodies began to be segregated. Instead of clothes made to fit the bodies, the bodies now had to be made to fit the clothes.

At the same time, when the flappers of the 1920s became popular, women could no longer hide any excess flesh under tucks and layers of draping. The fashions of the 1920s were lightweight and revealing. The answer to both problems? Dieting.

At this time, mothers began to be pressured to restrict the diet of their children. Dr. Lulu Hunt Peters advocated dieting for children. Concepts of gluttony and Calvinistic warnings to be frugal, saving, and spare played an influential counterpoint to the abundance in the country in this time. In the midst of plenty, people were afraid to indulge. But, in spite of the standard sizes for children and the pressure on parents to beware of making their children fat, most parents in the 1920s and 1930s thought baby fat was just that, and that it would pass.

e.   THE 1940s: FEAR OF FAT

By the 1940s, fear of fat was stronger. Fat was thought to be linked to polio. Many people thought wrongly that fat children caught polio more easily than thin children. Dieting then became preventive medicine.

Fat began to be linked to heart disease as well. There was no attempt to differentiate between those who were fat and healthy and those who were fat and also had heart disease. In the minds of the public, fat *caused* heart disease. This is a myth that continues today and is much more difficult to erase from the convictions of the public than the notion about polio.

Given such a dramatic and obvious "cause" of heart disease, drastic measures were understandable. Amphetamines were given as a treatment for obesity or even slight overweight condition in the 1940s, in spite of the American Medical Association's disapproval.

Fat began to be seen as an enemy so powerful that concerted action was necessary to fight back. Groups against obesity were formalized in TOPS (Take Off Pounds Sensibly) in 1948. Overeaters Anonymous followed in 1960 and Weight Watchers in 1961. This organized fight against fat was the result of greater interest in the psychology of the individual and the effectiveness of group therapy. As well as giving encouragement and support to members, weight loss groups often operated on a competitive basis (who lost the most this week?). Emphasis was on weight reduction, usually without exploring why a person was fat or whether they were unhealthy to begin with.

The Metropolitan Life Company contributed greatly to the public's misconceptions about a healthy weight. In 1943 and 1944, Metropolitan Life released their "average" height and weight charts. They were not average. They were strongly influenced by the prejudices of the company's statistician, Louis Dublin, who convinced the company to reduce the figures to a low "ideal" weight. There was no adjustment for age, puberty, or post-pregnancy for women. There was no adjustment for age or puberty for men.

These figures did not reflect American society. They held up as average what the Metropolitan Life Company thought should be ideal. The medical profession embraced this chart as the great commandment of dieting. "Thou shalt achieve the Metropolitan Life goals." Using these charts as a guideline, only thin people appeared normal and most people appeared overweight. More and more people began to believe they were overweight.

f. THE 1950s: ERA OF THE SUBURBAN HOUSEWIFE

The 1950s suburbia "utopia" had at its center a kitchen, presided over by a housewife who was aware of every calorie, every vitamin in each mouthful of food that went into her family's mouths. She was expected to choose, cook, and serve healthy, nutritious meals to her family — but not eat herself. She was the conduit of all good things, but she did not partake. She was expected to restrain herself from the tempting desserts that she made for the family; she was expected only to serve.

Magazines aimed at women buyers showed diets on one page and elaborate, rich recipes on the facing page. The housewife's life was one of self-sacrifice and rigid efforts to fit the model assigned her by society. She was expected to satisfy all her family's needs without ever having a need of her own. Women were caretakers, nurturers; no one nurtured them.

Women were expected to emulate the fast-selling Barbie dolls with their impossible figures and hard bodies. The slim waist, the tight hips were achieved in the fifties with the help of corsets and girdles. Even teenagers had elastic panty girdles.

g. THE LAST THREE DECADES

The women of the 1960s threw away the corsets and the girdles and created internal girdles with diet and exercises. No longer relying on plastic stays and elastic, women had to reconstruct their bodies from the inside. This took effort, money, and, of course, a new diet.

Metrecal! Magical Metrecal! In 1965, with a national ad campaign, the combined sales of Sego and the diet drink Metrecal were $450 million. It was the beginning of the multi-million dollar diet business which has dominated women's concepts of themselves and turned the diet industry into the $35-billion-a-year business it is today.

The pressure to diet starts young. Parents are pressured to prevent obesity in their children. In 1965, "experts" advocated dieting at 13, dieting at 5, even at birth, and some even demanded that mothers prevent obesity *in utero*. A quick look at a library shelf today shows this has continued:

- *Keep Your Kids Thin*
- *Help the Overweight Child*
- *How to Improve Your Child's Behavior Through Diet*
- *Kids' Slimming Book*

Dieting became a normal way of life. By the 1970s, diet foods were often regarded as "normal" foods.

At the same time, feminists began to inquire actively into women's place in society. They were demanding equality and interesting choices in society. It became a mark of rebellion *not* to be on a diet. Not dieting could be a woman's assertion of independence from male medicine and commerce, and from the self-punishing aspects of women's lives. Women began to look into why they were being pressured into dieting. They did not seem to inquire whether fat was necessarily unhealthy, but they began to look at why they ate and how they looked at food.

In 1983, the Metropolitan Life Company revised its charts to accept heavier weights as normal. That is not to say that the new tables are any more accurate than the old, for they still do not take into account individual differences: one individual's genetic history of cancer or another's genetic history of diabetes.

Today, as throughout history, women strive for the normal, the ideal. Men do as well, but the ideal for women is more restricting, more impossible, more unhealthy than the ideal for men. And it is getting worse. Gallup poll results show that in 1950, 44 percent of women believed they were overweight; in 1973, 55 percent believed they weighed too much; and in 1980, 70 percent (of college women) thought they were overweight. In 1990, close to 80 percent of all women thought they were overweight. Woman are still responding to the "ideal" charts and to the sophisticated and persuasive ad campaigns that tell us normal weight is abnormal.

h. CREATING THE PERSONAL IDEAL

1. The teen ideal

Today's women continue to pursue an impossible goal dictated by society. But when and how do we take the social ideal and make it a vital part of our life's goals?

Some women I talked to suggested that we create our ideal body image when we are teens. They suggested that whatever we decide is ideal when we are teens is the body image we consider ideal for the rest of our lives. Each generation measures itself against different ideals — Marilyn Monroe in the fifties, Twiggy in the sixties — and holds onto those ideals for a lifetime.

That idea disturbed me because I do not think I saw much choice when I was 15. My world was very narrow, my choices limited. How do teens decide on an ideal based on such limited experience?

Susan, a friend, a therapist, and a guest at the dinner party, said, "I think we evaluate ourselves on a criteria of whatever our generation says. Some of my clients see size four and six as ideal because they are looking at the standards of today. In my whole life I was never any less than size ten. I mean, to be a size four or size six was never part of my repertoire of possibilities. I wanted to be smaller than size ten, but not size four. Size ten was the standard of my teens. So when I feel too fat, it is too fat according to my growing up days, not too fat according to what is in the world right now."

On the other hand, it may be that we cherish our teen ideal and adopt the current ideal as well — perhaps the slim waist and curves of the fifties, and the muscle tone and no-hair-on-the-body of today. If that is the way we find our body ideal, if we add more requirements as we grow older, we create a more and more limited ideal. Perhaps we modify our original ideal, letting some dreams go and adding others — the bust can be smaller, legs longer, hips smaller and firmer, and today we can do without the tan.

2. Encouraging change

We do not have to remain slaves to the ideal we took on in our younger years. Most people are capable of amazing changes. If we do form a strong sense of our own body image during our teen years, and we do adopt our cultural ideal by fashioning a mental picture of what our own body *should* be at that time, we still are capable of modifying that image and accepting a more reasonable, comfortable image later in life.

After all, we do accept physical changes: limbs can break, our endurance levels change, women reach menopause. Sometimes we improve with time. We learn to type, to play the piano, to use our bodies differently. We could learn to accept a different ideal. But to do that, women must give serious thought to what they believe about their bodies, why they believe it, and what such a belief means to them. We don't always take the time to stop and consider ourselves this way.

5
CONTROLLING YOUR LIFE

a. BEING THE GOOD GIRL

Many women have been taught that to be happy they must please others. They must please Mom and Dad, must learn to be a "good girl." A good girl comes when she is called. A good girl eats everything on her plate. A good girl does well in school, doesn't lose her temper, is polite and cooperative. If she pleases others, she is praised, petted, and loved. She learns to please others in order to fit into a social group.

It is not hard at first. When she is little, a girl wants to do what pleases others. But by junior high, when she is about 14 years old, she discovers the cost of pleasing others. Because others want her to, she attends parties she hates, dates boys who scare her, and behaves in ways that make her uncomfortable. How much can she compromise her own beliefs to be accepted by the group? How much independence can she balance against estrangement from her parents? Leslie said, "When I was 16 I hung around this girl because she got dates. I changed my hair to be like her. Crazy. Everything is appearance at that age. I don't think it's until you get out on your own that you realize what you like to do and what you don't like to do. It's too bad that we don't try more things when we're home, when we're young and not afraid of failure."

Lisa, a sophisticated counselor, told me about the pull she felt between her parents and her friends. "As an adolescent I was not taught to value my friends. Even though I knew I needed them, caring for them wasn't encouraged. [My parents'] focus was on getting married, having men around ..."

Many adults find themselves still trying to please parents even though the very act makes the adult child unhappy. They are still searching for the acceptable compromise.

A young girl starts pleasing her parents, then her friends, her boyfriend, her husband. If a women is "good enough" at pleasing, she is promised affection, admiration, respect, and appreciation. In time her efforts to please others leave her with no time or energy to please herself, and often without any clear idea of how to please herself.

The needs of others change and their demands on her to be a certain person or look a certain way change. She reacts to their needs like a weather vane, spinning and changing direction to suit the prevailing climate. She loses pounds, changes hair style, buys new clothes, and exercises, trying to become what others currently demand. Because she is anxious to please everyone, she responds to the strong social demands of the media pressure. The media demands conformity to its standards and holds out extravagant rewards. It promises that if a woman is thin enough, fit enough, stylish enough, she will be admired, accepted, and sexually appreciated.

It lies. Once a woman depends on assurances outside herself for her vision of herself, she loses control of her life.

b. BECOMING A BETTER GIRL

As women, we are taught that if we are not happy, not secure, not sure who we are, it is either that we were born inadequate or that we are not trying hard enough to be perfect. We feel there is something wrong with us, not with the media or the social world around us.

In an effort to change themselves, women with great determination are able to bind themselves to cruel beauty regimes in order to sculpt themselves into someone they think will please.

We all have surprisingly similar ideas about what will please:

"firm, well-proportioned and glowing"

"physically fit"

"20 pounds slimmer and toned"

"15 to 20 pounds lighter with a smaller nose and neck"

"5 pounds lighter and more muscles"

"30 pounds lighter and no cellulite"

"thinner, firmer"

"healthy, athletic"

"36-22-35"

We are culturally conditioned to admire what the advertisers tell us to admire. We don't question why we admire it. We just adopt it as "normal" and "standard." But, in spite of the strict standards we set for ourselves, we don't judge our friends this way. We probably realize that, if we held such an impossibly high standard for our friends, we wouldn't have any.

Women spend time, energy, and money making themselves into something that will please others. Why? Because we think that no one will love us or appreciate us as we are — bare-faced, long necked, plump, short, our personality hanging out to be seen by anyone. As we are, we are not good enough.

How we reach that conviction is the result of a complex system of socialization aided by a biased and simple message from the media — consume products. Spend money. Buy! Buy! Buy! Buy our instant happiness — exercise bikes, exercise programs, fitness memberships, rowing machines, calorie charts, ultra-lite foods, "lite" beer, tummy trimming belts, perfect tennis shoes, smooth complexions, shiny hair, dark eyelashes, perfect lips, slim-fit jeans, flattering haircuts, make-over magic, seductive perfume, sculptured nails.

The messages are all around us, all day, everywhere. We are constantly told we are imperfect. If we want to be accepted, we must change, shape, reduce, remove — make ourselves different. To do that we must buy products. And, since perfection is impossible, we must continue to buy. In our constant pursuit of the perfect body, we devalue the one we have and negate the unique and intriguing person we are.

c. WHO CONTROLS OUR SELF-WORTH?

1. The boyfriend

Into these feelings of inadequacy rides "the boyfriend." The boyfriend is going to make a woman feel accepted, appreciated, valued. His warmth and understanding are going to make her "whole." She is going to feel accepted and valued because he accepts and values her. She will feel good because he "makes" her feel good. Her feelings are going to be controlled by the boyfriend. I am not suggesting that the boyfriend asks for this power. Many woman hand it over to him. They are culturally conditioned through years of pleasing others to look for someone to control their emotions. Leslie told me that she had experienced this problem in the bedroom. "I remember when I was engaged, my boyfriend said, 'What do you like? What do you want?' I didn't know. I wasn't a virgin. I'd had a baby by then, but I didn't know. I'd always looked at sex the wrong way. It was always one-sided — and never my side."

A huge responsibility now rests on the boyfriend. It is his job to care for the woman's feelings, her sense of self, her image of herself. She has been taught to please others. Any gratification she gets is a gift from others, not something she achieves with her own efforts.

In many instances, the boyfriend has similar needs of validation and reassurance and requires the girlfriend to support his feelings of worth. There may be some balance in such a relationship but it would be subjected to great misunderstandings and pressures. In situations where the boyfriend does not rely on others for his sense of self, he can knowingly or unknowingly become tyrannical. He pleases himself because he knows what makes him happy, and she pleases him because she thinks that will make her happy.

Years of practice at this relationship can lead to a situation where oppression reigns. As Teresa said, "He told her to lose weight, so she did. It took her six months and just about killed her, but she did it. Then he told her to do something about her sunken eyes."

Rhea said: "He told me to lose weight and he'd have sex with me again. So I did. I finally did. And then he wanted me to stop because he didn't want other men looking at me. And then, of course, he still didn't want to touch me."

To attract a candidate to fill the boyfriend role a woman makes herself alluring. She may assess the competition for boyfriends: what do other women look like, what is admired by most people, how can she be better? Then she may groom, clothe, and trim herself to fit an image of what she thinks will be "feminine" and attractive. She looks to advertisements to learn what is attractive to men. Some men look to advertisements to learn what should attract them. Advertisements are not two-way. Their message is one way only — from the advertiser to the consumer. And they constantly tell women that we are not good enough.

2. Family members

Not only the boyfriend is important in the "good girl's" sense of self. Her parents and family are still important to her. She is still trying to please her mother and will probably try to please her for the rest of her life. Some mothers can be pleased. Some mothers can never be pleased. Mothers are reported to have made the most devastating comments to their daughters. "You'd better get an education because you'll never attract a man." "No wonder you never go out. You're such a slob, who would want to be seen with you?"

Daughters, on the other hand, may invest a great deal of their own sense of adequacy in their mothers' opinions. So a woman with a boyfriend or husband on whom she depends for feelings of worth may also have a mother and family on whom she depends for feelings of worth. Geographical and some emotional distance allow the woman's need for her mother's approval to fade a little. However, correspondingly, her need for her boyfriend's approval may increase.

Lisa, a counselor, described how her dependency on others for self-worth carried over from her family life to her married life.

> I really think that women who have problems with low self-esteem, with eating disorders, take all that stuff and move it into whatever relationship they move into. It has terrible carry-over qualities. If you don't feel good about yourself...you transfer that into your relationships. And I see that very clearly now. My feelings about myself, the ones I worked out by watching my mother and figuring out what it meant to be feminine, and my weight and my body image...I just took from my family and fit into my marriage. I don't think I caused all the problems in my marriage, but I think I tolerated them because I didn't demand anything different.

If a woman's mother and boyfriend criticize her, and she relies on them for her value, she will be unhappy. If she relies on herself, she will not believe her mother and boyfriend and will seek different, more appreciative company.

d. CONTROLLING LIFE BY DEFINING OURSELVES

We attempt to make ourselves acceptable to others by describing ourselves as valuable.

1. Through work

Families change, work changes, relationships change, but our personality remains basically the same. Yet we do not define ourselves by our personalities. While we may not always define ourselves in

41

relation to men (for example, John MacGillvray's wife), we do define ourselves by our position in society, particularly our work position.

At my party everyone there defined herself by her work:

"I am an editor."

"I am a film producer."

And then through her family:

"I have a husband."

"I have children."

No one defined herself through her personality:

"I am a hedonist."

"I am aggressive."

"I am curious."

There is a difference between seeing where we fit in society and having no existence outside that designated role. It may be one of the present rules of our social group that we define ourselves by a work role. Such a social rule may be telling us that we are starting to value our work above all else in life.

2. Through bodies, not personalities

Some men are accomplished at distancing themselves from their partners, from all women. Some men are conditioned to look at women as sex objects, to rate them one to ten, ogling them on the street, rating sexual attributes that seem obvious — big bust, long legs, long, shiny hair.

We women are not necessarily better. Women also have learned to treat men as objects, rating "hunks" in a way that ignores the personality of the man and concentrates on his body, a sure way to create distance from the man inside the body. It removes real feelings from the relationship and sets up barriers to emotional understanding, to acceptance of the real person.

If the relationship depends on a body's appearance, then a partner sees great value in maintaining that appearance regardless of how distant that appearance may be from the real person. Two people with distorted or altered body image who are struggling to maintain their designer bodies will have a difficult time establishing an emotionally satisfying relationship. They may have matching sweat pants, exercise schedules, and diet plans, but they are unlikely to have accepting, loving, uncritical attitudes to each other. Their body images get in the way.

3. Through exercise

Many woman told me that they felt good about their bodies when they exercised, when they fit into what was socially expected of them, when their bodies were healthy, strong, and muscular, when they were seen as trying to be perfect. Women wanted firmer muscles, coordinated bodies, more exercise time, a regular workout.

No one mentioned specific activities that made them feel good about their bodies outside of exercising. No one said:

> "I feel good about my body when I'm standing in the rain and feeling a part of nature."

> "I feel good about my body when I am sexually aroused because the feelings of warmth make me feel sensuous, alive, and move me into a different world."

> "I feel good about my body when I'm breastfeeding and the milk comes easily, and my baby is contented."

> "I feel good about my body when I knead bread and the dough comes up between my fingers and my hands feel strong and useful."

In answer to the question "What do you wish you could change in your life," women said:

> "I wish I could regain a disciplined exercise program and a good diet."

> "I wish I could exercise more when I'm working."

> "I wish I could eat what I liked."

> "Exercise more."

> "I wish I could change my body."

> "Eating and exercise routine."

Most women relate their feelings about their body to weight and exercise. That is a narrow area of satisfaction and generally is only an area of dissatisfaction. Bodies do so much more than lose and gain weight.

e. RESENTING THE NEED TO CONTROL OUR LIVES

At the same time we want to be fit and slim, we want the pressure that created this need to disappear. The same women who answered above also said they thought that women's biggest problems with their body image were:

> "Too much emphasis on looks, not enough self-satisfaction."

> "Too little self-esteem and self-confidence. I feel that society expects a certain physical shape for all women."

> "A stereotyped perfect female body which means there is always something lacking in the individual — breasts too small, hips too large, feet too big. The perfect image is seen in movies, on television, and idolized by men through Playboy.... We're supposed to look like Barbie dolls, but very few of us really do look like this."

> "Weight. No question. I'm sure every woman has said once in her life that she wished she weighed less."

The pressures on us to be different make us angry and resentful and underlie our feelings of inadequacy. If we were acceptable to start with, we would not be trying to change.

Yet despite this resentment, we do not address the problem that seems fundamental to our feelings of acceptance, that by trying to be "good girls" and find universal acceptance, we have allowed control of our lives to move outside ourselves, to our partners, to our mothers, to the media, to society. We cannot be free of such pressures until we accept ourselves within a reasonable, comfortable body image, regardless of external pressures on us from anyone else to be different.

If we come from families that have a pattern of trying to please, where no one relies on himself or herself, and everyone depends on external reassurances, it is much harder to be sure of ourselves. It is hard to feel morally free to do what is best for us, to feel "right" when we choose to look after ourselves. Very often women have never thought about what is best for them.

f. KEEPING THE CONTROL IN OUR HANDS

We are not alone in the world. We do not have to isolate ourselves to find control over our lives. We don't have to take an adversarial position with others, swords high, battle shields ready. But we cannot give away the control of who we are, of how we see ourselves. Boyfriends, husbands, and friends can help us. Others can offer feelings of acceptance, of comfort, of understanding. Others can help us see ourselves more clearly and appreciate our worth. Lovers and friends can have a reciprocal relationship with us. They give us attention and appreciation as well as make demands. There is value in cooperating with people who matter as long as we don't give away our definition of ourselves.

As you work at regaining control of your own self-esteem, look over Worksheet #2. It gives some helpful strategies for dealing with criticism from others.

WORKSHEET #2
DEALING WITH CRITICISM

Once you are convinced that your body is quite wonderful, you will find that the criticisms of others merely annoy and don't cause catastrophic upheavals in your psyche. But until you can look at the critic and think "She's got a problem," not "I've got a problem," the following come-backs might help.

At home, with your partner

"Fat stores estrogen and estrogen contributes to a vigorous sexual life. You don't want me to lose that, do you?"

At home, with your mother and/or father

"Dieting makes a person sick. You don't want me to be sick, do you?"

"Stable overweight is healthier than dieting. Don't you want me to be healthy?"

"You're criticizing me."

"You're putting me down."

"That's a cruel remark."

"I'd appreciate it if you would stop criticizing me." (and then don't discuss it any more)

"You're criticizing me and I resent it."

In a store buying clothes

"My body's perfectly normal; your clothes are inadequate."

"I'm fine, your clothes aren't good enough."

With co-workers

"I'm happy, healthy, energetic and capable. How are you?"

"I don't diet."

"I don't talk about diets, diseases, or depression."

Give no excuses or reasons for what you do or do not eat. Do <u>not</u> say, I should or should not have certain foods. I should lose weight. Just don't discuss it.

If others comment on the morality of eating or not eating, change the subject. You'll get good at it.

At work, if your boss comments on your size

"Do you have a weight prejudice?"

"Do you think that only thin people can be healthy and capable?"

"Are you criticizing my work?"

If possible, be aggressive. Your boss's attitudes are not reasonable and he or she may be responding to a vague prejudice. Label prejudice as such. Educate your boss. Tell him or her the facts and see if you can change that prejudice. If that doesn't work, use the human rights laws to defend yourself. (Check which laws are applicable to you in your province or state.)

With friends

"Don't you accept me as I am?"

"Would you like me better if I were different?"

"I am more than just my weight and so are you."

It is difficult to come up with answers in every situation, but you can develop a few that work well almost anywhere. Use what suits you, what you feel comfortable with, what will make you feel as though you are making your point and maintaining control of the situation.

6

WEIGHT PREJUDICE

Western society has a strong prejudice against fat. Even worse, it has a strong prejudice against *people* who are fat.

This prejudice starts early. Kindergarten children think fat people are "bad." Parents teach their children that "fat is bad" and admonish them "not to get fat." Children incorporate this fear into their internal value system and create another generation of people whose greatest fear is that they will get fat.

Weight prejudice is now a social norm. It is all right to be prejudiced against fat and fat people. More people accept this prejudice than question it. Women who talk about dieting seldom question the need to diet or to be slim. They not only think "thin is good," but also "fat is bad."

a. THE ACCEPTANCE OF WEIGHT PREJUDICE

Many people believe that fat people could be slim if they just tried hard enough. Obviously they are not trying, so they deserve to be punished. A person who is fat then is seen as morally lazy. Many cruel and unhealthy practices then become "reasonable." It becomes "reasonable" to socially ignore fat people and not extend them the same courtesies others receive. It becomes "reasonable" to name-call, criticize, and treat a fat person like a child. It is part of our culture to humiliate fat people, "for their own good." Once most people accept such a prejudice, social behavior changes and it become acceptable to be cruel to fat people. Socially permitted punishments are meted out subtly and not so subtly. Fat people are ridiculed. They are held back from job advancement. They are less likely to be chosen as sexual partners. They are less likely to be accepted into their college. They are less likely to get a job. All this seems justified because advertisers have convinced us that everyone should be thin.

This harassment and ridicule verges on social sadism. While some of us do not actively persecute fat people, we usually remain silent while others do. Our silence is support for that harassment and persecution. If we peel off layers of justification, parroting advertisements and unsupported rationale, we come to the kernel of belief that most of society holds: that no one should be fat; that fat people should "do something about it."

A notice in an aircraft brochure made this prejudice clear: "Pregnant women, the mentally handicapped, and fat people cannot sit in the emergency exit of this plane."

How fat one wonders? Fat people are obviously considered immobile.

Jobs are harder to find in many areas, including teaching. Instead of considering large women as role models for children, hiring personnel accept the prevalent weight prejudice and try to create for children a world without large people, as if being large was in some way abnormal. Large women, rather than being seen as healthy, normal role models, are seen as bad models.

If weight prejudice continues to influence many hiring practices, we may soon have a world where none of our bosses are fat. That will "prove" that fat people cannot succeed. They will have less chance of success, not because they are incompetent, but because they have been systematically banned from having the chance to succeed. Millions of large women are restrained and limited by weight prejudice from taking a productive place in society. Society is poorer because it survives without their contributions.

Social pressure to lose weight is intense. There is more pressure to lose weight than to give up alcohol or drugs. Strangers feel free to advise an "overweight" woman on her diet, comment on her size and her clothes, make disparaging remarks such as "You have such a pretty face," and in general refuse to accept the whole person.

Because only 8 percent of the adult female population fits the impossible size ten, 92 percent of women are not "acceptable." To some degree, most women feel the weight prejudice of our society, most women feel unacceptable.

The situation is ludicrous. There is no inherent virtue in thinness. Fat is "immoral" because a multi-billion dollar diet industry says so. The diet industry spends million of dollars to bang into our heads the "truth" of this concept. They sell their products on the basis that fat is bad. As long as the buying public sees fat as morally and socially bad (physically bad is not as important), the public will keep buying the products they think they need to prevent or eliminate fat. The diet industry teaches the public to look on fat people as heretics to the religion of thin, as "weight sinners."

b. THE RELIGION OF THIN

Society believes that fat is immoral, that good, responsible people are not fat.

"Matter of Fat: Eating to win and to lose"

"Success Stories: Debbie D. and Lynne H. lost 133 pounds each"

"Image in Action"

"Snack Attack"

"Should You Drink Yourself Thin?"

"Confessions of a Beauty Sinner"

These magazine articles do not question the need to be thin. To be thin is to be intelligent, witty, powerful, accomplished, talented, sexually attractive, and, of course, healthy. None of that is necessarily true, yet magazines rarely question the basic assumptions they make about women's bodies. Readers rarely question those assumptions either. The implication in magazine articles, books, advertisements, movies, and song lyrics is that the body you have is not good enough and a thin one would be better. Most people believe thin is good with the unquestioning belief that they would bring to a religion. Why do people believe this?

Some theorists believe that since North Americans essentially gave up an inherited class system, it looks for ways of distinguishing different levels of society. Merit has come to be falsely associated with weight. If you are thin, you must have struggled to become thin, and, therefore, you deserve all the good things that come your way. If you are fat, you have not struggled and you do not deserve wealth, power, or social prestige. Therefore, thin people merit a higher social position than fat people.

Some theorists believe that as women enter the power structure of the work force they threaten the existing status quo. In order to keep the power community the same as it was, executive women must look like men, androgynous — no breasts, no hips — angular, and in male-imitation business suits so that they do not appear to change the structure of society at all.

50

The theory of power is a circular one since it feeds off itself. Because society imbues thin people with the qualities of intelligence, competence, and discipline, more opportunities come to those who are thin. Some women see thinness as a means to power, a means to manipulate society's attitudes to their advantage. A lifelong pursuit of thinness engenders feelings of worthlessness which make aggressive competition in the work world much more difficult and much less likely. In a sense, a woman enslaves herself in the pursuit of thinness, in the pursuit of failure.

Then there is the theory that the need to be thin is a need to be different from our mothers. She was self-sacrificing and a doormat, and we vow we will be different. We will be more like a man. Therefore, we will be thin.

Yet another theory is based on women's collective yearnings for independence. For the many women who are bound by poverty or by ties of motherhood or limited by a poor education, independence is a dream. In North America, money gives independence, so rich women are admired. Cher looks good to many women not just because she is tall and incredibly thin, but because by being thin, she appears to be rich and, therefore, independent.

Even in some forms of Christianity there is the embedded concept that our bodies, particularly women's bodies, are basically evil. In these religions, God sees humans as weak, unworthy, and constantly corrupt. Women growing up with this philosophy have to struggle to feel an inner sense of worth when those whom they trust continually tell them that they are evil and born to suffer. Such conditioning makes it easier for women to deny their own worth, to search for an impossible ideal, and to embrace the suffering of dieting.

Finally, there is the "waste of time" theory. If women spend much of their adult life in the pursuit of thinness, they will have little time, energy, or money to compete in the work force. They will be subjugated by their own impossible goals.

c. HOW SOCIETY VIEWS THE LARGE WOMAN

Many thousands of years ago when the world worshipped the Great Goddess, women were thought to magically produce children, without a need for men. At the time when women were powerful, dominant, and aggressive, when they were war-like and even demanded the human sacrifice of young men, large women were admired and important. Any woman of any size was admired and important.

There is a theory that in the deepest psyche of humanity, men fear a return of this ancient social pattern, and that one way to prevent such a role reversal is to glorify small and fragile woman and ridicule large women. If small women are the ideal and large women the exception, men need not fear women.

The problem with this theory is that it assumes knowledge of ancient history that most people do not have. While some people may believe that large women could be too powerful and that small women are easier to dominate, it seems unlikely that most people have an ancient motivating fear of the society of the Great Goddess.

Whatever our reasoning and whatever our collective past, it is obvious that North American society today has a cultural prejudice against large women.

Everyone needs a sense of self and a sense of place in society. For many big women, the problem of being large is compounded by the problem of being "invisible" to others. Because many people define size ten as normal, they see big women as abnormal. If they cannot accept the "abnormal," they refuse to see it. "They look past me, above me, to either side of me. They won't look at my eyes," says one big woman.

This is a typical prejudiced behavior pattern and relegates large women to the status of non-persons.

Our society ignores a woman with a large body. We advise her to dress in simple, conservative clothes, so that she will be less noticeable. We do not want to see her. We teach her to be polite, jolly, and inoffensive. We may accept some women of unusual talent in spite of the fact that they are large, but we do not celebrate their big and magnificent bodies as a positive part of their image and we do not extend this acceptance to all large women.

For a time, there seemed to be some hope in the black community that women would be revered for their contributions, for their stature. There was some hope that the black community would produce a broad range of ideal women — big and magnificent, short and plump, tall and broad-shouldered — women who accomplished things, who led the way for others. It looked as though a new ideal might emerge. But black women, white women, Asian women, and

Native women are all attracted to thinness. We seem united in our pursuit of the impossible.

d. FASHIONS FOR LARGE WOMEN

From the social attitude that large woman are not normal, are ugly, and should be ignored, come frumpy, dull, unobtrusive, "matronly" fashions. Given our society's emphasis on looking good, and given women's desire to be accepted as looking good, fashionable clothes become an important way of joining the normal group.

Clothes make a statement —

- that we belong to a certain social class (skin-heads have definite clothing restrictions, as do business executives)

- that we have a certain occupation (the nurse's uniform, the bus driver's uniform, the layered clothing of the bag lady, the executive suit of the lawyer)

- that we respect ourselves (our clothing is clean, fashionable)

- that we consider ourselves sexually attractive

Fashionable clothes contribute to a woman's self-confidence. We generally feel better, more capable, and more competent if we feel well-dressed. This is a result of very strong social conditioning. Clothes have been evidence of social values for hundreds of centuries.

Clothes can be crippling if we spend more than we can afford, or if we feel unacceptable unless we are perfectly dressed. But, generally, clothes are not physically harmful the way diets are. In the history of the world, clothes are one way that men and women express their personalities uniquely and creatively.

Given the vast satisfaction to be derived from attractive clothes, it is unfair that large women are restricted by lack of choice in the fashion market. Not only are large women made to feel abnormal, they are, for the most part, denied the chance to experience the transforming magic of attractive clothes.

I interviewed Rita, a 58-year-old owner of a fashionable dress shop. She has a regular group of customers who return season after season and she knows them well. I asked her why women buy clothes.

"To fill a need in their lives. To feel better about themselves. Most women want clothes that make them look younger and thinner — especially thinner."

I asked Rita if she thought attractive clothes made the changes in a person's self-esteem that magazine ads promised.

"I have seen people change because of the way they dressed. I have seen people become more confident. In good business suits, for instance, they felt confident enough to take new responsibilities, take opportunities."

I suggested to Rita that perhaps the confidence came after the woman invested money in herself, after she proved to herself that she was worth spending money on. She might then believe she could get the job she was dressing for.

"Or the life-style," Rita said, "or the holiday, or whatever she's after."

Recently, large women have been dressing with more flamboyance, more individual expression of personality. This hint of change in fashion focus comes from an enlivening sense of personal worth. Large woman are important. Large women are valuable. Nancy Roberts in *Breaking All the Rules*, gives a good example of the opportunities for individual taste and expression in clothes. Although this attitude is rare, it springs up in small pockets of enthusiasm in Canada, the U.S.A, and Europe. Generally, most shops and fashion stores do not promote large as attractive. Larger women must shop with relentless fervor to find flattering, fashionable clothes.

e. WHAT IS OVERWEIGHT?

According to author Nancy Roberts, 47 percent of British women are size sixteen and above. The percentage of women in North America size sixteen and larger is unlikely to be much different. Therefore, 47 percent of women are not small. Yet size sixteen and above is not considered normal by our society. Forty-seven percent of our female population is abnormal? Ridiculous.

If you are over size fourteen, society says that you are overweight, fat, or even obese. The words are relative, subjective, and used indiscriminately to describe a variety of shapes and sizes.

The term "overweight" means different things to different people. Is anything over size fourteen "overweight" in our culture? Is a person "overweight" if they are heavier than the insurance charts say they should be? Physically, a person may be very healthy at 30 pounds over the "recommended " weight. Are they then "overweight" if that weight is a healthy, natural weight?

"Fat" is equally relative. Those who try to trim "fat" from an apparently thin body are just as convinced they are fat as those who live with 50 pounds past their 20-year-old weight. And how fat can a person be before she is obese? Does your doctor call you obese when your are 30 pounds over the weight recorded on her chart? Or does she call you obese when *she* is 10 pounds over her "ideal" weight and worried about the weight of the world in general?

We do not seem to try to establish an individual usual, healthy weight. If you have been 145 pounds for 10 years of your adult life and have been healthy at that weight, why would 155 pounds be overweight? If you were 145 pounds at age 20 and 155 pounds at age 50 that would seem to be quite an acceptable weight increase. But if 155 pounds is 30 pounds over the ideal chart, does that make you unhealthy?

If you were 150 pounds at age 20, 165 after your last pregnancy and you seem to stay between 175 and 180 now at age 50, why wouldn't that be a healthy weight for you whatever the charts said?

Why can't we forget the charts and the "averages" and apply our own standards to what is normal and healthy for each woman? We need to establish our individual standard weight, a natural, non-dieting weight.

Each woman needs to ask herself —

- What weight (give or take 10 pounds) does my body try to maintain?

- Does my body weight allow me to move easily through life?

- Can I walk, dance, swim, make love, play baseball, tap dance, do what I want to do at this weight?

Perhaps we should define fat and overweight as the weight at which we are not able to function well, at which we have little energy, little body flexibility, the weight at which our body gets in the way of our activities.

An older woman I know was a size ten during her twenties, thirties, and forties. At menopause she began to put on weight. Now, at age 79, she is about size fourteen or sixteen and plump, "matronly." She eats whatever she likes, has never dieted. She can stroll ten miles without puffing. She gives dinner parties for 16 without being fatigued. She travels, goes to concerts, goes dancing, and generally uses her body to enjoy life. Her response to her increased weight at menopause was not to diet. Her response was to buy bigger, fabulous clothes so that her plumper body was still attractive. Why is this sensible attitude so rare?

f. SET THEORY OF NATURAL WEIGHT

Each person has a natural weight that her body prefers. It may be thin, it may be heavy, but it is the weight her body hovers near when she eats three meals a day and exercises normally (that is, without a heavy exercise regime, or a jogging schedule, just the moderate exercise of daily living). If she does not starve or binge she will probably maintain this weight through trials and stress, happy times and sad, within 5 to 15 pounds (2.3 to 6.8 kg).

Each person has an individual set of genes inherited from parents so that her tendency to plumpness or thinness comes to her from generations before her. When I worked as a public health nurse, a father brought his three-year-old son into the clinic. The father was worried about his son's small size. We talked about the child's eating and illnesses, but I finally reassured the father that some children had to be in the lower 25 percent of the chart and that his son seemed healthy. When I stood to escort the father to my office door, he stood as well. I looked over his head. He might have been 5'4" (163 cm) tall. What was he expecting from his son?

In the same way, inherited characteristics influence a woman's natural set point or natural weight. Her natural weight may or may not be fashionable. Society's reaction to her natural weight is not part of the set point. Her body is not defending fashion; it is defending health and function.

A dieter knows that she can lose those first few pounds quite easily and then have a hard time losing any more. Her body tries to protect her from starvation and its debilitating side effects so it defends the set point by becoming more efficient at metabolizing food and trying hard to keep the weight the body knows it needs.

Bodies also defend themselves against overweight but not as strongly since overweight is not the same immediate physical threat to the body that underweight is.

There is some evidence to indicate that the body's natural weight is the weight at which the individual is biologically most healthy and that the reason the body defends itself from losing or gaining is to protect health.

When an individual eats three regular meals a day and does not diet, she responds to hunger appropriately. She knows when she is hungry and when she is full. On the other hand, when a woman depends on a book of rules or a diet counselor, something or someone outside her body, to tell her what to eat and when, she loses the ability to know when she is hungry or full. She may no longer trust her body's feelings of hunger or fullness. She looks for authority outside herself, a new diet, a doctor's opinion, her husband's demands, her children's criticism, the latest article in a magazine.

The women who answered my questionnaires told me that they were afraid they would balloon out of control if they didn't watch their weight. These were women who had been dieting. Often they had dieted for years or were dieting now. Those who felt their bodies would not balloon, but would stay a stable weight, had not been dieting. Perhaps we have to trust our bodies to maintain a natural weight for a time before we can believe they truly will do so.

g. "BUT FAT IS UNHEALTHY"

We live with many myths about weight and overweight. We hear myths that sometimes seem to be backed by informed opinion and so we often accept as true statements that have no truth behind them at all.

In trying to educate North Americans about the need to eat nutritious foods instead of junk foods, the health profession has over-simplified the prescription for health. Eating "well," exercising regularly, and keeping your weight at "ideal" on the charts is not necessarily a formula for longevity. Millions of products are sold on the philosophy that fat is an enemy to health, that any regime that keeps fat off your body will give health. This is not necessarily true.

Myth #1: Fat will cause a person to die early.

When compiling statistics on the relationship between overweight and death, many studies combine the severely obese with people less than 30 percent overweight by their "ideal" chart. Such studies apply the problems of the severely obese to those who are only slightly overweight. In this way, the hazards of the severely obese are considered in these studies to be the hazards of the slightly overweight. It is much like lumping people with a slight cold in with people with viral pneumonia and declaring the hazards of death to be the average of both.

Myth #2: Fat causes heart disease.

Not true. There is simply not enough evidence to say that fat causes heart disease. Obesity without the complications of diabetes, smoking, or high blood pressure does not show a definite correlation to heart disease. If a person has symptoms of heart disease, then obesity may become a contributing problem. But obesity or overweight does not *cause* heart disease. Eating sugar will contribute to the problems of a person with diabetes; but eating sugar does not *cause* her diabetes.

Myth #3: Fat causes cardiovascular disease, such as hardening of the arteries.

This is not, in itself, true. Cardiovascular disease is related to weight gain, heredity, and fitness levels, not to consistent overweight or obesity.

Myth #4: Fat causes high blood pressure.

Again, high blood pressure is more likely to be related to overeating than to a stable overweight. Dieters who starve, then overeat are more likely to have high blood pressure than people who maintain a constant overweight.

Myth #5: If your doctor advises a diet, you need to diet.

Doctors are often profoundly ignorant about body image, weight acceptance, the effects of dieting on health, and the effects of weight on health. Doctors are often as confused as patients about the health status of heavy women. Doctors are, after all, members of society and are subjected to the same learned weight prejudices as the rest of us.

h. ADJUSTING REALITY TO FIT THE MYTH

Weight prejudice is so common that most people don't even question why they are afraid of becoming fat or why they look critically at large women. Most people ignore the influence of weight prejudice around them and adjust reality to fit their prejudice.

A friend and I read the same article about women serving in the armed forces in the Gulf War. There were several pictures accompanying the article. My friend was struck with the fact that many of the women were big. "Must be junk food," she said. I protested that many women are naturally big. She was used to seeing pictures in magazines that reflected only one thin body type, and while she understood intellectually that women came in different sizes, she had not accepted it. She saw normal physical types as abnormal if they did not fit her ideal of size ten. Weight prejudice is so strong in our society that we see the prejudice as the reality. In many ways, every day, we treat normal people as outside the norm because they don't fit an artificial ideal.

The consequence of this weight prejudice is to encourage the useless pursuit of thinness with its wide weight swings, gains and losses. Such wide weight swings may be responsible for many of the illnesses that have previously been attributed to overweight itself.

Weight prejudice causes not only unhealthy dieting practices, but misery, unhappiness, and frustration for millions of women. Women are afraid to stop working toward the "ideal" because most women fear fat. We are afraid to accept ourselves at a larger size than is fashionable. Giving up our goal of size ten means accepting that personal larger size and most of us will not do it. We want the impossible tiny dream. We do not want to stop trying.

i. SOCIALLY ACCEPTING DIFFERENT SIZED BODIES

Carole Shaw, editor of the magazine *BBW* (Big Beautiful Women) said in her February, 1991, editorial, "....the large-sized person's 'problem' is not a result of overeating but of society's overreacting."

It is difficult indeed for women to believe that statement even when it is obviously true. Large women are victims of the social conditions everyone absorbs and they are often the first to blame themselves for being themselves. In order to change at least some of society's view of large people, these women must accept themselves. Since large is a relative term and many women consider themselves large and fat at weights from 100 pounds up, all women need to learn to accept their natural weight as normal and good whether or not it fits into the social norm.

Imagine this. You turn on the eleven o'clock national news. The woman giving the news is short and plump, calm and intelligent. She is more interesting to listen to than anyone else we know. She never giggles, or acts "sexy," kittenish, or coy. She is aware of her intelligence and her contribution to the TV station. She is well paid for that contribution.

You switch channels to the symphony. The conductor is a brilliant woman, large and impressive, who brings from the orchestra sounds you couldn't imagine that orchestra capable of making. No one comments on her size. Everyone comments on her talent.

Channel 2 is broadcasting a concert by a well-known folk singer who sings such beautiful songs that no one comments on her large body. No one considers that her size is detrimental to her art. No one wants her to change. It might damage her music. What she produces makes her beautiful, whatever her size.

This is not such an impossible dream. We already have some large women who are publicly acclaimed for their talent: Rita Mac-Neil, folk singer; Jessye Norman, opera star; Marianne Sagebrecht, actor; Ronnie Gilbert, singer, formerly of the Weavers; Choncata Ferrell, actor; Dianne Schuur, jazz singer; Jackie Torrence, actor. These big women are all judged and admired for what they are, not how they look. There are big women in our own lives who appear happy and successful: the loans officer at my bank, an artist friend, my aunt, my mother. We all need the freedom to be beautiful in a way that comes naturally to us.

7

UNDERSTANDING THE HAZARDS OF WEIGHT PREJUDICE

Weight prejudice conditions us to accept some bizarre behaviors. Self-imposed starvation would appear peculiar if weren't called dieting.

a. THE DIETING MYSTIQUE

Dieters are by far the most numerous casualties of the war with the perfect size ten. The principle method of reconstructing your body image in our society is to diet. In spite of the fact that 98 percent of diets fail (the dieter regains the weight plus some within one year), women continually diet, searching for the fantasy body that they are sure is hidden within them. Dieting is so common now that not only do most women diet, dieting is seen as a "normal" eating pattern.

Whatever the diet — oat bran diet, "sensible" diet, carbohydrate diet, fat-free diet — it is a method of restricting food temporarily. For a few weeks or a few months the dieter watches what she eats and involves herself in an elaborate moral game of "good" food and "bad" food. A dieter's sense of worth becomes dependent on how much food she eats and/or what kind of food she eats. She reconstructs her body from the inside to please not a healthy concept of her individual weight but an external social myth that has promised through the latest ad to give her health and happiness.

A dieter hops on her scale in the morning, or seven or eight times in the day, to find out if she is "good." She responds to her scale as if it were a critical god, telling her that she is "good" today (she lost weight), or "bad" today (she failed to lose weight). Intellectually, she may know her exact weight is unimportant, but emotionally she depends on it.

Dieting may make her feel better because dieting is "feminine" so she feels more feminine when she diets. Dieting may make her feel better because she is accomplishing a goal she has set for herself and therefore feels more in charge of her life. Dieting may make her feel better because she thinks it is supposed to make her feel better. Also, women who have been successful in other areas of their lives believe that they can be successful at dieting. They do not consider, or do not understand, their body's powerful ability to protect itself from starvation.

A slim body is imbued with magical qualities. It will get the dieter love, sex, marriage, children, a job promotion, money, travel, whatever she wants. The fantasy is so strong and so seductive that dieters, even after 20 years of repeated failures, continue to diet.

Dieting is almost a subculture in North America. Dieters understand a specific body of knowledge. They research new information on the subject. They have developed their own jargon and are united under an almost religious belief in the power of a slim body.

Many dieters accept a variety of ideas without considering how valid these pieces of information are.

- Brown fat cells burn less efficiently in fat people.
- Certain groups of food should not be eaten together.
- Eat brand name nutrient bars with prescribed food additives.
- Counting calories is passé — exercise the weight off.
- Avoid fats.
- Diets high in fiber will cause you to lose weight.
- Competing in weight loss with others helps you lose weight.

All these statements belong in the realm of folk lore. None of these statements should be the basis for any action at all. But lucrative businesses operate on such magical slogans.

b. DIETING AND HEALTH

Dieting is not the road to health. Dieting will not necessarily make a woman physically better. It will probably make her physically worse. And, of course, 98 percent of women will gain back the weight and more, so the dieter will probably be less healthy and still be heavier than she wanted to be. But, generally, we do not diet to improve our health; we diet to look good. Health is only incidental to looking good. The aim of most dieters is beauty.

We used to be taught, in the medical world, that reducing would help prevent diabetes in older people. Some studies now indicate that an older woman who maintains a stable "overweight" is less likely to develop diabetes than one who diets and puts her body through the stresses of weight loss and weight gain. It may be that it is the changes in weight that cause the problems, not the weight itself.

In the same vein, middle-aged men with a family history of heart disease might also benefit from maintaining their usual weight and balancing their usual eating patterns with an exercise habit so that they do not gain weight. Yet thousands believe that losing weight is vitally important to preventing heart disease in all people. No one guarantees that dieting will prevent heart disease, yet thousands believe it.

When I worked as a public health nurse in the 1970s, our nutritionist asked us to remind patients that the heart of a fat person had to pump a high volume of blood through miles of extra blood vessels and, therefore, added stress to the heart. This conclusion came out of the weight prejudice of the time, not out of medical fact or common sense. It was wrong. The heart is a muscle. Exercise makes it strong. The heart of a fat person is not necessarily weakened by the extra miles it pumps.

1. The stress of the weight loss/weight gain cycle

The dangers of dieting lie in the stress of weight gain and weight loss and the lack of a stable weight. The fluctuations in nutrition and starvation can result in low blood pressure, hair loss, gallstones, muscle fatigue, fast or slow heart rate, anemia, gout, nausea, and swelling of the feet and hands. The effect of dieting on the body depends on how fast the dieter loses the weight, how much weight she loses, and how much nutrition loss the body suffers. While more research needs to be done, it seems that the health hazards to our bodies are related more to the drastic weight fluctuations we put our bodies through when we diet than "overweight" alone.

Because we as a society do not accept bodies that are not "ideal," we force healthy large women into dieting. The diet produces weight gain as well as physical illnesses that formerly were thought to be a result of obesity. Now we are beginning to understand that such illness may not be the result of obesity at all, but the result of dieting.

But doctors prescribe diets. I know they do. One wonders how they can when they know that diets have a 98 percent failure rate and will probably increase the patient's problems. If they prescribed a regime for tuberculosis that had a 98 percent failure rate they probably would lose their license. But we accept such erroneous advice because the doctor is a victim of social pressure just as the patient is. She, although she may understand intellectually that diets do not work, may have an emotional need to see this patient reduce. "Fat is bad."

2. Losing the inner thermostat

One of the dangers of dieting is the woman's loss of internal regulation of hunger and fullness — de-activating the internal hunger thermostat. A dieter depends on her diet sheet, a written schedule, an outside cue, to tell her when and how much to eat. Internal feelings of hunger and fullness — the body's way of protecting its stable weight — are ignored. A dieter must intellectually tell herself what to eat, how much, and when. Because she depends on the diet sheet, she eats in a rigid manner ignoring other needs in her life. She ignores stress, social pressures such as a company dinner, and her own emotional needs. Through the conditioning process of dieting, the dieter deactivates her internal control and loses her protection from weight loss and weight gain. She trades a self-regulatory responsive system for an externally controlled one.

There is probably no better way to get fat than to diet. Dieting tells your body that you are starving. The wise body immediately becomes more efficient and uses more of what you eat, wasting less. When you start eating normally again, your body prepares itself for the next starvation period and stores the food as fat and you gain weight.

3. Drugs

And then there is the jumble of drugs: over-the-counter drugs and prescription drugs. Drugs are generally seen as a way to lose weight fast. Losing weight fast is, in itself, a threat to health.

There seem to be mainly two kinds of over-the-counter diet pills. Fiber fillers, with vitamins and minerals, are taken with fluid (water or milk) in place of meals and are supposed to give you a feeling of being full without adding calories. Fillers with benzocaine also give you a feeling of being full, and the benzocaine, a local anaesthetic, slightly numbs the stomach and its hunger pangs — at least, that's the theory. By using these aids a woman suppresses her own natural signals of hunger.

Amphetamines, which used to be prescribed often in the 1960s, are less likely to be prescribed today. Like many other diet aids, they are ineffective or at least not more effective than counting calories. They can also be dangerous, especially when combined with particular diets that lack essential elements.

Drugs have been prescribed for reducing for centuries, probably hundreds of centuries, from the diet pill of the Byzantine in the third century B.C., made of sesame, honey, oil, almonds, and sea onion, to the "Slim Mints" of today. Women have been promised a slim body and the magic of a Cinderella's life if we only pop pills. Every time a woman takes a pill to reduce her weight she is reinforcing the idea that she is not good enough as she is. While the pills themselves may be physically harmless (and they may not be) the psychological conditioning wears away at a woman's self-esteem and makes her less likely to accept herself.

c. EATING DISORDERS

The pursuit of thinness has led approximately seven million women and one million men in North America into the dangerous world of eating disorders — anorexia nervosa, bulimia nervosa, and compulsive eating — according to information from the National Association of Anorexia Nervosa and Associated Diseases in Highland Park, Illinois. Anorexia nervosa is a state of self-enforced starvation that is some people's solution to their fears. Bulimia nervosa, a binge-purge cycle of eating and vomiting, often with periods of fasting, is used even more commonly by people who desperately need to control the world around them. Compulsive eating, although often lumped with eating disorders, is more difficult to define since it has many of the aspects of bulimia: binge eating, preoccupation with food, constant eating accompanied by guilt. The women who label themselves as compulsive eaters point out that they do not purge, vomit, or take laxatives.

A woman with an eating disorder focuses her life on food — eating, not eating, purging, exercising to burn off food, calculating how much food she can eat and how much food she can burn off. Food becomes almost a poison that she tries to avoid.

1. Anorexia nervosa

Women who suffer from anorexia nervosa may be obvious since they are very thin. The danger of such thinness is often overlooked in families where a high value is placed on being thin. "She's done so well. She's lost thirty pounds."

A starving woman may receive compliments from family members on her will power and ability to lose weight even when her health is dangerously compromised. Weight prejudice blinds many people to the dangers of the problem. Many people believe thin is healthy.

Women with anorexia suffer tremendous hunger and deny themselves food. They feel that every bite they take results in fat. They tell me that they can see their stomachs bulge after eating a half a muffin. They may know exactly how many calories are in each mouthful of food and precisely calculate their low daily intake. Normal feminine curves look like the enemy "fat" to them, and they are relentless in pursuing a body that is almost a skeleton covered with skin.

Because an eating disorder satisfies emotional needs, women with anorexia do not respond to reasonable arguments for weight gain. They are convinced that they will be happy *only* if they are very thin.

Women with anorexia usually have a distorted body image. They may look in the mirror and see fat where there is no fat. They may see what they feel — as fat when they are depressed, acceptable when they are happy. Lisa, an insightful, 29-year-old woman said, "I might feel thin in the morning and eat something for lunch and feel huge. I have such an incredible distortion of what my body image is. And even though I can be very rational about this, still, you know, it is distorted."

2. Bulimia nervosa

A woman who suffers from bulimia sees herself as not being good enough as she is — too "fat," too "lumpy." Like the woman who is anorexic, she wants a perfect face, a perfect figure, a perfect body. She thinks that if she disciplines herself, diets, exercises, she will become perfect. When she does all she can and is still not perfect, she takes stronger steps to achieve perfection. She starves herself. Then, in reaction to the starving, she binges. She takes laxatives and may even compulsively exercise. She drives herself to a state where she spends most of her time and energy feeding or not feeding herself, caring for the body that she hates. She restricts food and then overeats in a chaotic response to her needs and fears. In spite of all her efforts to be perfect, she is never satisfied with how she looks.

She equates happiness with looking good and, in her own mind, she never looks good enough.

It seems that people with bulimia are, in general, intelligent and often successful in other areas of their lives. The women I interviewed were warm, compassionate, and courageously trying to deal with their problems. They were often aware of the extreme emotional and physical swings in their lives but unable to stop them.

A woman with bulimia hides her preoccupation with food. She may buy hamburgers at six different fast food outlets so that no one restaurant waitress knows how much she eats. She may buy a great deal of food and pretend she has family in the car waiting for it. She can be so clever at hiding her problems from others that her parents or her husband can live with her for years and not realize that every day she eats and vomits. She is ashamed of her bulimia and ashamed of her body. She is not the perfect person she wants to be.

3. Compulsive eating

Women who classify themselves as compulsive eaters are usually very large and have for years dieted and focused on food. They see themselves as much like their sisters with bulimia with the exception that they do not purge. They have similar difficulties in coping with their emotions.

4. An emotional problem

Women with eating disorders think about food most of the day, how to get it, when and where they can eat it, how they can purge it, how they can hide it, how they can afford it. Yet people with eating disorders do not have fundamental problems with food; they have problems with unacknowledged emotions. Underneath their drive for physical perfection, their control of their eating, is a bubbling cauldron of emotions they have never faced. In that simmering pot may be —

- anger towards their mothers

- their reaction to the sexual abuse of their childhood (the latest estimate is that 66 percent of those with eating disorders were sexually abused as children)

- their fears of rejection, loneliness, or even happiness

A woman with eating disorders deals with all these uncomfortable and sometimes violent emotions by ignoring them and concentrating on her weight. She cannot tell anger or fear from hunger — everything is hunger.

Many people who suffer from eating disorders are enmeshed in a fight to have some control over their lives, some power, and they choose eating or not eating as a way of getting some power. It may be the only area of their lives that they can control. This soon rebounds on them for, after a time, they cannot stop their disorder and it controls them.

d. SURGERY

There are other methods of trying to become thin that seem barbaric but are practiced in North America. A woman phoned a counseling agency and asked if a lipectomy was a good treatment for her teenaged daughter's weight problem. Her doctor was recommending it and the mother had heard that people sometimes died from the procedure. It's a little like asking, "If I lock my daughter in her room and don't let her eat for a month, will she lose weight?" She probably will, but she may die in the process. A lipectomy, the removal of part of the fatty tissue, is a greater threat to the daughter's health than overweight may ever be. Some people have their jaws wired to prevent them from eating. Some have their stomach stapled to keep them from eating much at a time. Some have intestinal bypass surgery so that their body cannot absorb much food. All these procedures are dangerous. When you consider that most often the underlying problem with the person's weight is either emotional or social, physical intervention seems useless. And usually, it is useless.

e. UNDERWEIGHT

When we read about diets we seldom read about the dangers of being underweight. When was the last time you saw a caution against underweight accompanying a diet plan? Besides the obvious dangers of being anorexic, we seldom talk about the problems of being so thin that the body has no reserves when sickness depletes the body even further. We do not talk about the dangers of osteoporosis in older women. A light body does not stimulate density in the bones as well as a heavy body, and an aging body needs bone density. Aging women store estrogen in the fat on their hips, and estrogen helps keep the body young. An older woman may well be healthier if she is heavy than if she is thin. But do the magazine articles and diet plans talk about this?

f. "OVERWEIGHT" AS A PLUS

No one talks about the advantages of being "overweight." A woman will be physically healthier if she maintains her stable "overweight" than if she puts her body through the stresses of dieting. A woman who has a stable overweight, who does not diet, will have more time to enjoy life. She is not torturing her body with unnatural diets, drugs, or surgery. She is not forcing herself to vomit, nor is she compulsively thinking about food every minute of every day. She is not so thin that her body lacks resources to fight illness. She may have a healthy body image because she is not constantly reminding herself that she is not good enough. She is not continually failing at dieting. She is free to like herself.

We may understand intellectually that an obsession with weight is not good for us, that a healthy individual weight is better for us than a cultural ideal weight, but we may not be able to accept this on an emotional level. We want to be thin for the same reason women in China bound their feet. They had a strong social need to do so. We have a strong social need to be thin. In some ways we are like members of a religion who are asked to accept on blind faith the idea that women should wear a chain on their ankles with a heavy ball attached. A woman with unfettered ankles then becomes unfeminine in that culture. A woman who does not diet, who does not work hard to be thin may be considered unfeminine, unacceptable in our culture. Women may choose to be fettered, restricted, limited, and subjugated in order to "belong." That need to be part of the group, whatever we sacrifice in health, is strong.

Now try examining your own attitudes toward food and eating by completing Worksheet #3.

WORKSHEET #3
ASSESSING YOUR EATING HABITS

	YES	NO
1. Do you eat when you are not hungry?	❏	❏
2. Do you eat more than you want (e.g., finish the food on your plate even when you are full)?	❏	❏
3. Do you weigh yourself every day? Every week? Every month?	❏	❏
4. Do you count calories?	❏	❏
5. Do you think about food and eating as a negative part of your life?	❏	❏
6. Do you wish you could stop eating?	❏	❏
7. Do you think that if you ate less you would be thin?	❏	❏
8. Do you think that if you ate to satisfy your hunger you would be fat?	❏	❏
9. Do you usually eat between meals?	❏	❏
10. Do you eat regularly (three or four times a day)?	❏	❏
11. Do you leave food alone between meals?	❏	❏
12. Do you know what food groups are recommended by federal health agencies?	❏	❏
13. Do you know when you are hungry?	❏	❏
14. Do you eat when you are hungry?	❏	❏
15. Do you believe that your body will maintain a stable, constant weight if you eat three meals a day and satisfy your hunger?	❏	❏

If you answered no to questions 1 through 9 and yes to questions 10 through 15, you are probably happy with your body, probably do not diet, and understand and use food with comfort and efficiency.

If your yes and no answers are mixed for questions 1 through 15, you probably need to get a firm understanding of what an adequate and nutritious diet is, what your hunger feels like, and how you can satisfy your hunger and your body's nutritional needs without swinging from diet and starvation to binge eating back to starvation and again in a frantic attempt to be satisfied.

A regular pattern of eating a variety of foods results in a stable weight and less weight gain than yo-yo dieting.

8

CHALLENGING THE MYTHS

a. THE MYTH OF CONTROLLING OUR BODIES

As a society we have an amazing ability to take an idea and spread it quickly throughout our whole population. We can discover a fact in Tuktoyaktuk and transmit it to Albuquerque in a very short time. Advertisers grab such information, amplify it, and spread it further in support of their products. We are often the recipients of pieces of information that are incomplete, inaccurate, and misleading. In time, we come to accept such pieces of information as facts. It is easy to believe something we hear over and over. Myths become facts in our minds.

1. Health

In the 1960s, the western world began to look at fat as "bad." Mothers were told that they were responsible for overweight children because they allowed them too much fat. Two percent milk became the "ideal" milk. It gave us vitamins and minerals without too much fat. But, when mothers fed two percent milk to infants, the babies drank much more milk trying to get the calories and fat they needed. So, instead of reducing the fat the baby got, the two percent milk just increased the volume the baby had to drink to get the nutrients he or she needed.

Today we continue to respond in this way to isolated pieces of information, creating health regimes without understanding the consequences to our bodies.

Presently we are being told in "health" magazines, newspapers, even doctor's offices that cholesterol is bad for us. Yet cholesterol is necessary for the formation of natural steroids. Cholesterol is necessary for the formation of estrogen. When ads and articles tell us to reduce our cholesterol, they do not tell us what the total effect on our body will be. It is important, generally, for our western population, particularly for our middle-aged males, to try to eat well and exercise so that their bodies deal with the fat they eat. We are looking for high levels of high density lipoproteins (HDL) in the blood and low levels of low density lipoproteins (LDL) (both are types of cholesterol). Admittedly, fat and cholesterol are a problem for many. But cholesterol is not a poison, nor is it unnatural. It is difficult for us to understand what amount of fat and what kind of fat is necessary for health and what amount and kind of fat causes us harm.

The physiology of the body is not completely understood, so it is still possible for enthusiasts to proclaim nutritional "truths" without instant correction from medical and nutrition experts. It is often hard to refute some ads. The ad may say that reducing your cholesterol level will reduce your risk of heart disease. For people who have a genetic disposition to heart disease and who already have a high cholesterol count, this may be true. In the same sense we are told that controlling our sugar intake will improve our health. For people with diabetes who must constantly monitor the sugar content of their blood, this is undoubtedly true. The problems arise when a specific recommendation for a specific condition is generalized to apply to everyone. Individual differences, genetic predisposition, and unique adaptation influence the body's health, so detailed diets and formulas for health are difficult to prescribe.

Mental health is often directly related to physical health. That is, poor physical health can cause psychological deterioration, and poor mental health can cause physical ill health. When we are happy, we tend to be healthy. But happiness is a by-product of many activities and because these activities are many and varied, health is a complicated process. This is acknowledged but not precisely understood, so another "health fact" becomes shadowy, unpredictable, and uncontrollable.

2. Body size

Why do we think that if we follow a strict diet plan, exercise plan, and activity plan we will be guaranteed health and a thin body? Life is too full of uncontrollable variables to allow such strict control on our bodies. We may eat "healthy" food, brush our teeth regularly and yet have many cavities because we did not have fluoridated water as children. Cavities are not a moral fault. We are not "bad" with terrible eating habits because we have cavities in our teeth. We are unlucky. Fluoride treatment and good dental care help us, but strict control of our eating and exercise could not have prevented cavities.

While that logic seems obvious when applied to cavities in our teeth, we somehow cannot transfer that kind of thinking to body size.

It is a commonly held opinion that body size is controllable; that a woman is fat because she does not eat "properly." Like all general statements, there is a little truth in it. If a person did not eat at all, she would lose weight. She might die, but she would probably lose weight first. If appearance is more important than health, then a person could lose weight by starving herself into ill health. So, perhaps it might be partly true to say that a fat person could lose weight by dieting — if you ignore her health.

Many women do ignore their health. They have their jaws wired, undergo major intestinal surgery, starve themselves in other ways, and force themselves to be thin. The cost is enormous in health, time, energy, and money, and the result usually temporary. But that element of truth — that if one did not eat, one would lose weight — is exaggerated into a "health principle" so important that all other aspects of a person's size, weight, health, and happiness are ignored.

3. Aging

After the age of 30, we begin to notice the changes in our bodies that come with age. At about age 40 we notice that our eye muscles stop accomodating to distance the way they used to. At about 45, women usually begin menopause and their estrogen level decreases. With the decrease in estrogen, arteries have less protection from arteriosclerosis and the process of aging. Without estrogen therapy women can also suffer a dramatic loss of bone density in the four to five years immediately following menopause, leading to osteoporosis and fractures.

By the time we are 70, our hearts pump less blood per minute, our kidneys take longer to filter the blood, our lungs take in less air in a deep breath and therefore less oxygen, the tissues around the chest harden so we are unable to take as deep a breath as we used to. Our white blood cells gradually become less efficient at clearing out our systems, particularly our respiratory system. We have fewer taste buds on our tongue. We have less acute hearing, especially at high pitches. While we may be as intelligent and retain great ability to solve mental problems because we have developed many inter-connecting synapses, we may be slower to make decisions, possibly because we have more information to search through.

While our life expectancy has increased from about 47 years in 1900 to about 78 years for women, our bodies still age. Our increased longevity is primarily due to better preventive health measures, better nutrition, better immunization, and much more efficient treatment of disease. We are also more likely to have a comfortable old age because medical care is more effective. What used to be endured can now often be treated.

We have no way of stopping the aging process. Anyone who uses bifocals knows that her body changes. We accept changes in our eyes and compensate with glasses. We allocate no blame to anyone for the changes in our eyes. We do not consider ourselves weak-willed, self-indulgent, lazy, or undisciplined because we can no long read fine print.

But we do not accept other changes in our bodies with the same grace. We do not see loss of elasticity in our skin as inevitable. We reach for new and better creams and surgical face lifts. We do not see the gradual shifting of the body's contours as inevitable. We reach for magic diets and liposuction. We do not see a loss of some physical abilities as a natural part of aging. We frantically exercise harder and take megavitamins. We try to control our bodies, to deny the changes, and to strive for a magical impossible ideal.

b. HEALTH

1. Confusing information

It seems only reasonable to eat "healthy" foods, to stay away from junk foods, and exercise so that your body has a good chance to be healthy. This commonsense approach to health is blown apart by our ignorance. We are never sure which foods are "good" for us and which are "bad," which vitamins we need at what dosage, how much exercise, and what kind. We are told to include fiber in our diet to prevent cancer, vitamin C to prevent colds, folic acid to prevent menstrual cramps, vitamin B complex to prevent PMS, calcium to prevent osteoporosis, and low-fat foods to prevent heart disease.

We have confusing choices. How much calcium do we need from what sources? Is a calcium pill as good for us as calcium in milk? How can we know what kind of food is "good" for us when our heads are full of isolated pieces of information about food, food supplements, and food additives. To compound our problem, "experts" give us more advice on the elixirs of youth, the key to longevity. And we are faced with a collage of definite statements that sound authoritative and scientific but may only be advertising in disguise.

When we read ads, statements such as the following are presented as if they were the whole truth and as if the writer were determined to educate the reader.

"If blood cholesterol is lowered by 1 percent a person reduces their risk of heart attack by 20 percent."

That statement may be true if applied to a patient with high blood pressure who is genetically at risk of heart disease. It is not true for most of the population. It appears under a doctor's name in a foreword to a cookbook for low cholesterol meals and is commonly attributed to a doctor who studied the effects of a cholesterol-reducing drug. There are no studies to prove that high cholesterol in the blood causes heart disease or that low cholesterol prevents it.

In December, 1990, a national women's magazine published the article from which the following quotes are taken:

"Less is better. When it comes to fat....Experts contend that *any* fat, whether 'good' or 'bad' is at fault when it comes to boosting your risk of heart disease, cancer and a host of other maladies."

That extravagant, unsupported, false claim is qualified later on in the article.

"....cholesterol is actually essential to life."

In one paragraph the author tells us that any fat is bad for us, while in another tells us that fat is essential to life. No wonder readers find it hard to make informed decisions about food!

So what can we believe? How do we educate ourselves when we do not have time to go to university for a degree in nutrition, when we must pick up our information quickly in two-minute snatches from magazines, radio, and television.

2. Analyzing the information

It might be useful to devise a couple of questions that we can apply to advertisements.

(a) What are they selling?

(b) What would the world be like if everyone believed this ad?

A beer ad is a good example. The ad shows young people enjoying themselves at a party. There is a lot of beer. Everyone is drinking. Everyone is having fun.

What are they selling? Overtly, beer. Covertly, fun. The ad implies that drinking beer makes you have fun.

What would the world be like if everyone believed this ad? Almost everyone wants to have fun, so everyone would drink beer as much as possible. Beer at work, beer at every party. Your young children drinking beer, your parents drinking beer, you drinking beer. Society would be in chaos. We have enough trouble with alcoholism and the effects of alcohol in society now when only a small percentage of the population believes they must have beer to have fun. If everyone believed it, society would be constantly drugged.

Try those questions with an ad for a diet program. The diet program asks the dieter to drink "Formula Z" for three meals a day instead of eating.

What are they selling? Overtly, an idea, and some vitamins and fiber. Covertly, beauty, social acceptance, sexual attractiveness, change.

What would the world be like if every believed this ad? Most people want to be beautiful, accepted, sexually attractive. Many people are bored and want change in their lives. So, most people would give up food and drink Formula Z. Your children would not grow; your parents would get ill; in fact, people would be ill most of the time. We would lose the color, texture, aroma, and enjoyment of eating. Eating would not longer be a social occasion. Imagine Formula Z for Thanksgiving dinner, Formula Z for Christmas, Formula Z for your lunch with friends. Everyone drinking Formula Z and no one eating. We would all be quite ill. We would have no energy for the second great principle of today's health regime — exercise.

c. CONTROLLING OUR BODIES THROUGH EXERCISE

We are encouraged to exercise three times a week with our heart rates over 120 beats per minute (depending on our age) for fifteen minutes in order to prevent heart disease. We are told that daily exercise is even better so we will be stronger, look younger, and live longer.

1. Our obsession with exercise

For years we have been told to "go for the burn." Thousands of exercise programs tell us to work out so we can "look good." Fitness ads on television tell us we can have the body of a 30-year-old when we are 50. Friends tell us how wonderful they feel after jogging four miles every morning. Millions of people feel obliged to insist that they have a regular exercise time because scheduling a regular exercise time is a personally responsible thing to do. For the rising executive, it is almost important enough to be included on her resume: "I exercise three times a week and swim four miles a day."

There is, naturally, a good case for exercise. Of course a firmly toned muscular body allows a person to do more physical work without fatigue and strong muscles beside the bones protect the joints so a person can keep joints injury free. Many studies show that regular, moderate exercise can reduce the possibility of heart disease in some people and increase a person's chances of surviving heart disease. Regular exercise provides a time out of a busy schedule to relax, meditate, and relieve stress. Exercise is supposed to increase the endorphins in the brain giving the exerciser that feeling of well-being that follows a "good" workout.

Regular, moderate exercise can delay the incapacitating consequences of aging. Regular exercise allows your heart and lungs to work more efficiently, giving you greater energy and strength than if you did not exercise.

All are very positive reasons for exercising. But regular exercise will not change your genetic predisposition to heart disease.

Regular exercises takes time. It often adds stress for people with an already crowded schedule. Exercise is socially isolating and can allow an isolated individual even more time alone. Someone who avoids intimacy may spend most of her non-working time exercising.

Strenuous exercise gives the body no greater benefit than moderate exercise. Strenuous or competitive exercise carries the possibility of injury and strain to joints and muscles. Exercise combined with dieting can lead to bone mass loss and fractures.

Exercise, because it is seen as "good," can become an obsession, drawing a person into a rigid and sometimes compulsive activity that is used as a substitute for family time, socializing, exploring, or learning. If a woman exercises one hour every day, she spends three and half months in ten years exercising. What else could she have done with that time? Is that what she wants to do with that time?

2. Putting exercise in a healthy perspective

Magazines articles on diet and exercise, fitness and the body beautiful tell us how to shape and reshape our bodies, how to find our own diet style, our own exercise style as if it were the responsibility of every woman to be slim. They do not question the assumption that slim is best. In an article on how to lose that last ten pounds of "extra" weight, nowhere did the author suggest that your body may be trying to protect your health by maintaining a natural, individually desirable weight. The assumption is that women of determination and willpower can overcome the enemy "fat" and control their bodies.

In some magazines the diet and exercise regimes of famous people are examined:

"_____ is a vegetarian who eats raw fruit, vegetables and whole grains, nuts and beans. She walks four miles a day, five times a week. She exercises with a rowing machine, treadmill and stationary bike. She also jumps rope, skis and plays tennis."

"_____ eats fresh fruits, vegetables, seafood, salads, sushi and milk. She goes to aerobic classes and uses a personal trainer at home. She exercises two hours every day. She loves to run. She also works at free weights and rides a dirt bike."

This compulsive, semi-starved individual is held up as "successful." Rich, probably, but successful? Do we really want a life that requires two hours a day in exercise in order to keep our bodies admirable? We could spend those two hours a day listening to our school-aged daughter read, volunteering at the counseling center, learning Chinese, writing a novel, planting a garden, training a Labrador retriever, playing scrabble with our teen-aged son, listening to music, writing letters, making love. There are other choices in life.

This constant pursuit of thinness may be a prescription for a boring, insolated, unrewarding life.

Assess your attitudes toward exercise by completing Worksheet #4.

WORKSHEET #4
ASSESSING YOUR ATTITUDE TO EXERCISE

Cardiovascular fitness, the exercise the heart and lungs theoretically need to prevent heart disease, differs from muscular fitness, which is a state of physical development that results in muscular strength. Strength may feel good and be useful, it may help prevent joint injury, it may be admirable, but in itself it doesn't prevent disease.

Even the benefits of cardiovascular fitness are medically debated. Some studies indicate great benefits, some studies indicate no benefits, and some studies indicate benefits for a few. Presently, the medical community leans toward encouraging cardiovascular fitness as a way of diminishing the risk of heart failure. But it does not seem to be the magical immunization against heart disease for all that some researchers would have us believe. It probably helps most people. Having said that, and assuming that an increased fitness level may be healthy, answer the following questions.

	Yes	No
1. Can you accomplish the tasks of daily living with comfort: at work, at loving, at play?	❏	❏
2. Do you partake in activities that are strenuous enough to raise your heart rate to 120 beats per minute for fifteen minutes three times a week?	❏	❏
3. Do you think that if a person is thin she is fit?	❏	❏
4. Do you think that fat people are not fit?	❏	❏
5. Do you think that fat people cannot play active games?	❏	❏
6. Do you think that regular exercise will make your body more acceptable to you?	❏	❏

	Yes	No
7. Do you think regular exercise will improve your health?	❏	❏
8. Do you think regular exercise will prevent disease?	❏	❏
9. Do you think the time you spend regularly exercising will increase your social contacts?	❏	❏
10. Do you think the time you spend regularly exercising will be socially isolating?	❏	❏
11. Do you think the benefits of regular exercise will outweigh its drawbacks?	❏	❏
12. Do you think regular exercise will slow down your body's aging process?	❏	❏
13. Do you exercise primarily so that your body will look good?	❏	❏

Answers:

Questions 1 and 2: If you answered yes, you are probably fit.

Questions 3 through 6: These require "not necessarily" answers. Many thin people are not fit; many overweight people are fit. Many overweight people play active games; many thin people do not. And regular exercise may not make you feel more comfortable with your body; you may exercise compulsively in order to become thin. You may have a distorted body image and see yourself as fat and unacceptable whatever your size or weight.

Questions 7 through 11: The answer is "perhaps." If regular exercise results in increased strength of the muscles around your joints and you find you have less joint pain, and if regular exercise results in activities that get you out of the house and meeting people, or cooperating with others in a sporting event, or regular exercise seems to make you more alert mentally and interested in others and in activities, then regular exercise may improve your health.

But if regular exercise is an isolating experience that removes you from others, if it is strenuous and causes cracks in your bones, if it becomes a time burden that adds stress to your day, then it probably does not improve your health.

What seems to be lost in our health recommendations is the unique nature of an individual. Each of us has our own needs and requirements. An activity that is helpful and advantageous for one person may not be so for another.

Question 12: The answer is no. Regular exercise will not slow down the aging process. You will still have trouble focusing on small print. Regular exercise may increase your comfort because it may allow you to do more without fatigue as you age. You may retain a greater range of motion in your joints and so have more comfort in movement. However, it will not affect the genetic process of aging. What regular exercise may do is make that process more comfortable for a longer period.

Question 13: The answer to this question is important to you. Remember that you are an individual. What is a serious health risk to one person, may not be a serious health risk to another. Assess what your needs are in health and in exercise and adjust your life to satisfy those needs. Do not exercise because exercise benefits someone else.

If you answer yes to question 13, you are caught in the grist mill of social pressure that takes individuals and attempts to grind them out in an identical size and shape. Consider that you may exercise forever and never believe that you look good enough.

9
HOW TO FIND A COMFORTABLE, HEALTHY BODY IMAGE

a. WHAT IS HEALTHY EATING?

Nutritionists generally recommend the Canada Food Guide, or something like it, as a basis for healthy eating. This guide was first devised in 1942 and updated in 1982. It incorporates the nutrition recommendations for Canadians adopted by Health and Welfare, Canada, and is considered by nutritionists and medical practitioners to be sensible, safe, and reasonable. It is also flexible and leaves a great deal to the taste, judgment, and common sense of the individual. The U.S. Department of Agriculture with the U.S. Department of Health and Human Services puts out similar recommendations in "Nutrition and Your Health: Dietary Guidelines for Americans." You can usually get pamphlets and advice on nutrition from local health units.

The Canada Food Guide (included in Appendix 1 in this book) is simply written and easy to follow. Notice that it gives many choices, no restrictions on which foods to eat together, although there are assumptions that, for instance, two glasses of milk would not be taken all at once but at different times during the day. The guides recommend taking food in three meals during the day or three meals plus a snack. It assumes we will eat more or less food on different days, without affecting our weight or our health very much. This is a general guide, not a rigid one. A general guide is more useful to us than a rigid one because it is more realistic and reasonable, and allows for individual changes. It does not tell you what kind of fruits or vegetables to eat, for instance, just to eat four to five servings a day. It also acts as a guide rather than a manifesto.

The new Canadian "Guidelines for Healthy Eating," due to be released as this book is being released, will be even less definitive. Basically, the new guide recommends that we —

(a) enjoy a variety of foods

(b) emphasize cereals, breads, other grain products, vegetables, and fruits

(c) choose low-fat dairy products, lean meats, and foods prepared with little or no fat

(d) achieve and maintain a healthy body weight by enjoying regular physical activity and healthy eating

(e) limit salt, alcohol, and caffeine*

The problem with the general food guides, from a dieter's point of view, is that they are not weight loss diets. They are guides for healthy living, not necessarily slim living. The food guides seem too permissive, not demanding enough, not bossy enough. They do not require a huge commitment of energy to stay within their recommendations; they are too easy and the dieter does not have to suffer enough to follow them. Many people feel that they could not possibly lose weight if they eat normally.

b. WHAT IS A NATURAL WEIGHT?

A natural weight is the weight which your body wants to defend. It is determined by your genetic composition — if your family is short and stocky you will probably be that way as well, by your activity and fitness level and by your diet. Most women know what weight, give or take ten pounds, that their body tries to maintain. It is only reasonable, healthy, and sensible to accept that weight as normal for you.

A woman who follows the Canada Food Guide may lose weight if she is above her natural weight when she starts to eat three meals a day from all the recommended food groups. If a woman is close to her natural weight she probably will not lose weight. Her body, after all, tries to maintain her individual natural weight. Regular eating habits with a variety of foods will maintain that weight in a healthy state. The body is not concerned with how it looks, only with how it functions.

A woman must eat normally until she knows what her natural weight is, and then adjust mentally to accept herself at that weight. It sounds simple, impossibly simple, and seems to be just common sense, but it is not easy to do, nor is it commonly done. Women find eating normally and accepting their natural weight very hard to do. It feels like giving up and being irresponsible.

*From Health and Welfare, Canada

One of the most insidious pressures on women to be thin is the argument that they are ruining their health and must lose weight in order to prevent heart disease. In spite of the fact that this is definitely false, almost everyone believes it. Certainly your mother, your spouse, your children, and your coworkers believe it. You believe it. Your doctor may even believe it. The pressure on you to be a "responsible" adult and at least try to be thin is tremendous. You may have to face that pressure. If you have normal blood pressure and normal blood lipids and do not have diabetes, you risk more health problems losing weight than you do by maintaining your present weight. Turn the pressures around and inform those who are pushing you that they are advising a treatment that is dangerous to your heart and it is *they* who are being irresponsible. Defend the body you want and are comfortable with.

c. ACCEPTING YOURSELF

You know your natural weight, you follow a reasonable, normal diet, and you exercise moderately. You don't worry about your precise weight in pounds (or kilos), but you have a good idea at what point your body is most functional and comfortable. That weight does not fit the ideal.

The pressures to conform, to continue dieting and pursuing the impossible ideal are great. Your own social conditioning makes it difficult for you to like yourself the way you are, and the social conditioning of others makes them feel fully justified in harassing you to change "for your own good."

Many people are afraid to give up their quest for the ideal size ten. They feel unwomanly, lazy, and irresponsible if they don't try to be thin. It is not unusual to feel like that. You may be intellectually prepared to accept yourself at 140 pounds (63.5 kg) but emotionally you may still try for 115 pounds (52 kg).

How can you accept yourself? It is first important to try to understand as much as you can about the pressures on you —

(a) to be different from what you are

(b) to be slim

(c) to diet

(d) to exercise beyond reason

By reading this book, you already understand much better why society imposes these pressures on you and why it is so difficult to break free of them, even when they are obviously wrong. You may have come to understand yourself better, and can more easily see why you follow the dictates of society.

If you are so dissatisfied that you think of yourself as a "floating head," a well-groomed face, attractive hair style, completely divorced from the rest of your body, you are not alone. Many people respond to their bodies that way. It is a way of accepting only what you can and ignoring what you can't.

It is hard to recognize that it is not you who are abnormal or "bad"; it is society that holds odd and morally skewed views. Once you recognize that it is not your weight or shape that is bad, wrong, unhealthy, or unattractive but your attitude to your weight, you can look at yourself with more tolerance and more acceptance.

If you see yourself as a failure as a woman because you didn't succeed in achieving delicacy, dainty bones, and a wasp waist, then you will be constantly reminded of your failure and suffer from feelings of injustice, persecution, and hopelessness.

If you see yourself as morally weak or deviant because you are not as thin or as muscular as your think you *should* be, you may have difficulty presenting yourself socially in a positive way. You then may have trouble getting positive feelings back from society which makes it even harder for you to like and accept yourself.

To be free, to be confident, to grow in personality and character, we need to accept ourselves as we are and not berate ourselves for not being someone different. We have heard that advice every since we first started to read Ann Landers or *Seventeen Magazine*, but it is surprising how we ignore it. It is hard to accept our bodies when society tells us —

(a) feminine bodies do not have the social power or prestige of masculine bodies

(b) we are too tall, too short, too fat, not muscular enough to be beautiful

(c) we are the "wrong" race or color

My group of friends discussed this.

Jean: "The challenge is to see the beauty in yourself. It is very delusionary to base your sense of self-esteem on how you look."

Anne: "I think beauty comes from inside. It's always amazing to me how *anyone* can look beautiful when they're having an affair. People say, 'Have you lost weight?' and you want to say, 'No, I'm just having this great affair.'"

Susan: "We don't have a vocabulary other than losing weight or gaining weight for describing how we look. We don't know how to say, 'Oh, you seem so energized. I've never seen you looking so alive.'"

Carol: "I know a woman who is really quite wonderful and she says to people, 'You look like you've been taking care of yourself.' That is a compliment. Whatever it is, enough rest, enough pleasure, it looks good on you."

Women need to develop ways of looking at themselves to evaluate how they feel. Too often we relate everything to how much we weigh.

d. FINDING HELP

Learning to accept yourself is not an easy task, especially if you have spent years believing you were unacceptable. You may need help.

1. Therapists

Your own therapist, private counselor, or psychologist can help you to think through your attitudes about weight, help you understand your need to be size ten. Be sure to shop for a therapist who has some experience with weight prejudice, perhaps a therapist who has experience with women and eating disorders. A therapist with this kind of experience will have worked out many of the problems of weight prejudice.

A counselor provided by your workplace may not be helpful since the workplace pays your medical insurance and the health personnel may be strongly influenced by the prejudice and erroneous data on weight put out by their insurance company. Community therapists, who may be more independent, are not always covered under a medical plan, so check yours.

Question what your adviser is selling. If your adviser is a counselor in a weight reducing clinic, she has a vested interest in making you believe you need to lose weight. Any advice from her will be founded on that prejudice.

I had a long discussion in a mall coffee shop with a weight clinic counselor. She told me that I probably had gained only a pound a year over the last ten years and that I could take that pound a year off quite easily.

"Why should I?" I asked. "I thought I was healthy and attractive as I was."

She looked at me. She had never considered that some people do not want to lose weight. It was an interesting moment.

Susan, a therapist herself, and a guest at my dinner party, said, "I spent a lot of years feeling fat. And, at the time, I really wasn't fat. When I started to learn about what was going on behind my problem with weight, I found that it never had anything to do with actual fat in terms of numbers on a scale, or size of clothes. It was that every time I had a feeling about something, I translated it. If I felt scared, I was fat. If I felt angry, I was fat. If I felt happy, I was fat. If I felt sexual, I was fat. I think that when we say 'I'm too fat,' it has nothing to do with the weight. It's just that we don't know how to express our feelings. We don't know how to give our feelings names. We don't know what they are."

Such a strong denial of emotional life may lie underneath many women's need to be thin. It would be helpful to understand that if it is so. Such understanding could give a woman the freedom to accept herself. A good therapist can help with that understanding.

You probably know that continual dieting is harmful to you, so if you persist in continually dieting you must have a strong need to do it. A therapist can help you find that need and help you look for ways of satisfying it that don't involve dieting.

2. Nutritionists

Again, a nutritionist who has had experience with eating disorders is perhaps the best choice since she will have a good understanding of weight loss and weight gain as well as weight prejudice. A nutritionist can help you make reasonable, practical decisions about weight loss and about food. Nutritionists work in health centers, clinics, and private practice. You need to shop for a nutritionist who will be useful to you and who is well informed on the problems of weight prejudice. A nutritionist can be a good source of information and practical advice. Her services also may not be covered by medical insurance.

3. Support groups

I attended an eating disorder support group whenever I could for a year. The women were kind, understanding, and accepting. They knew I did not have an eating disorder, that I was writing about weight prejudice, and they were concerned that I not only understand their difficulties but that I have a chance to talk about anything that was bothering me. I felt accepted there. The therapist in charge of the group encouraged the women to make our Wednesday evening meetings a safe place to be.

There are therapist-directed support groups for women with eating disorders and women who are compulsive eaters, but it is difficult to find a group for women who don't yet have those extreme responses.

A support group without a therapist is less useful. Support groups without a therapist can deteriorate into competitive races: "My story is worse than your story"; "My weight gain is greater than yours." Or into complaint sessions when everyone shares problems in a way that leaves the participants not only trying to deal with their own problems but trying to solve other people's problems as well.

While a listening and supportive friend can be extremely helpful, a therapist often can be a catalyst for change, a mentor, a guide. It would be most helpful if you had a supportive, listening friend, a therapist, a nutritionist, an appreciative partner, and an uncritical mother. A dream environment!

e. THE HAZARDS OF CHANGE

Many people will not understand how someone can be content at size eighteen. She will meet weight prejudice at work, at home, when relatives gather, and when she shops.

If we give up our efforts to be size ten, we pay a price in social censure:

"You're not trying."

"You have such a great personality. Why can't you lose a little weight?"

"You have such a pretty face...."

On the other hand, we free ourselves and give ourselves time, energy, and money to develop other areas of our life. Consider how you want to spend twenty years — in pursuit of the unattainable size ten, or accepting yourself and developing your interests and talents.

It is sometimes easier to be comfortable with a big body, or a short or tall body, if we know and respect others who are built like us. It would be easier still if the successful women we knew close to us were big, if our bank manager was big, our teacher at night classes, our doctor, our hair stylist, the beauty counselor at the department store. We need these people to be not only big but confident about being big.

When you decide that you can accept yourself as a big person, remember that you may be the only one who considers that you are big. Because we are inundated with thin women as role models, many women consider themselves too big at size ten.

Consider the response I received from a small, probably size eight, woman. She wants to be thinner, more muscular, and taller. She had been thin in high school and all through college. She has an interesting career, is married, and has two children. She is still thin but she is not happy with her figure.

She said, "Magazines make me feel angry about the expectations placed on women to look like the models portrayed. Most men I know expect women, or at least their idea of the woman *they* want, to look like this. *I* want to look like those beautiful women and I often *do* feel incompetent — that if I tried harder, maybe I *could* look like that.

"I wish Barbie dolls had never been invented and that healthy bodies, whatever their size or shape, were considered beautiful. I would really like women's bodies to be celebrated for what they are — life-giving and nurturing! Not only as pixie-like 18-year-old nymphs."

Women need to work at changing what they view as admirable. We need to see ourselves as beautiful in many sizes and shapes. We can do that.

Try completing Worksheet #5 and see if you can start to change your own body image.

WORKSHEET #5
CHANGING YOUR BODY IMAGE

1. Think about your positive attributes, the things about yourself you do not want to change. Write them down and label them List A.

2. Think about what you'd like to change about yourself. Write these attributes down and label them List B.

3. For each item in List B, ask yourself the following questions:

   a. Is it possible to change this?

   b. Is it a reasonable goal to change this?

   c. How long would it take?

   d. How much would it cost —

   > in time

   > in money

   > in social discomfort

   e. Is it worth it?

4. For each item in List B, ask your self these questions:

   a. Why do I want to change this?

   b. What pressure do I feel to change this?

   c. What benefit do I expect if I change this?

   d. Do I have any other options?

   e. Will changing the items in List B affect the items in List A?

5. What is your ideal body image? Is it a set of measurements (112 pounds, blond hair, dark eyelashes) or a set of adjectives (a reliable, useful, resilient body that is unique and comfortable)?

   Is your ideal body image a reasonable one? (If you ideally would like to be 5'10" and you are 5'2", your ideal is not reasonable. Similarly, if your ideal size is size 4 and you are size 14, that is not a reasonable body image for you.)

   Is your ideal body image possible?

6. What difference do you think achieving your ideal body image will make in your life —

   a. at home

   b. with your family of origin (mother, father, brothers and sisters)

   c. at work

   d. socially

Write these benefits down and think about them. Do you just have a vague idea that "things will be better" or can you imagine exactly what the reactions will be?

When you have this picture in your mind of what life will be like, ask yourself —

Will my partner really be more interested in me?

Will my children really care?

Will I have to suffer to attain that body image?

Will my family have to suffer?

Will I be comfortable with this image when I achieve it?

Will I be able to maintain it without sacrificing all my time and energy?

Will I be healthy?

Will I be satisfied?

Adjust your body image until you have a practical body image that you believe you will be comfortable with, will be able to maintain without suffering, will be healthy and able to work, play, and love without severe restrictions.

7. What difference will achieving your ideal body image make in how you feel about yourself? Will you —

   like yourself better

   be more confident

   be more talented

be more capable

be more loving

be more accepting

be more honest and straightforward

be more real

Cinderella dreams aside, what will you be able to do then that you cannot do now? Why can't you do what you want now? Is it your body that is preventing you from getting what you want, or is it your attitude to your body?

A "perfect" size and shape does not create talent, competence, and love in spite of the advertisers' promises. Your self-esteem is dependent on your attitude, on your acceptance of yourself as you are, not on your size. Consider what size and shape you naturally are and work on accepting that as good, normal, and beautiful.

10

FIGHTING FOR CHANGE

Women want to occupy their space like a rock — solid, unequivocally secure, unaffected by the winds of social opinion. We want to be seen, recognized, appreciated, and admired. Well, why not? We want to know ourselves from within, feel acceptance from within, and gain our confidence from who we are, not from the recognition or acceptance we get from others.

It is very hard to be that secure in the kind of social climate most of us live in. Weight prejudice is insidious and difficult to combat.

But we do not have to accept that social bias forever. Women are capable of great changes. We have qualities of compassion, understanding, intelligence, and heaps of common sense. We can stop wars, clean up the environment, end racism. We *can* change the social concept of weight prejudice and the thin ideal.

a. THE WAR WITHIN

I asked women what they thought was the biggest problem women had with their body image.

An artist told me that she thought the biggest problem was, "the contradiction between being a successful, powerful woman and a beautiful, admired fluff-head."

A medical student told me, "I wish women would worry less about what they look like to strangers and concentrate on more interesting things, like communications with friends, doing interesting things. I think the biggest problem with women is their preoccupation with their body. If women stopped talking about it perhaps it would become less of an issue.

"What frustrates me most is how important our image is when we look for respect and power in the work force. We are so concerned that if we look feminine and voluptuous then we aren't a serious contender at work. I'm sure Danny DeVito wouldn't go to work in a corset, wig, and platform shoes because he was concerned that his coworkers wouldn't take him seriously as a fat, bald, short man."

The women I'm quoting here had to deal with pressures from society to be small, thin, and always beautiful. Most women do have to fight those pressures. Some do so successfully. They ignore the ideal and happily seek their own level of comfort. Some do so less successfully. They resist dieting but secretly consider that they are not really good enough to be a woman. And some are overwhelmed by the social pressures and their obvious deviation from the social ideal and spend a large part of their lives trying to achieve a narrow and dangerous concept of what is right for them.

These pressures make some women very angry. A 35-year-old mother and college teacher told me, "We are taught to loathe our bodies if they don't conform to an ideal. We are bombarded with manufactured images on TV and in advertising that show us how we should look. We're taught that we can't have any natural odours — they're offensive. We're taught that our only commodity is sexual attraction, not brains, guts, hard work, or compassion."

This angry reaction to the restrictive body image is common among women. What do women do with that anger? Some fight the social ideal and accept themselves as good and desirable. But many women do not. Many women feel helpless against such strong pressures.

We are not helpless. We *can* change society's attitudes. We changed the nineteenth century child labor laws, after all. We can make changes individually. We can correct false statements in our families, at work, and in social situations.

We can start by changing our attitudes about size. We can educate ourselves about a healthy and reasonable body shape and weight and then resist family and social pressure to conform to unreal standards.

We can clothe our big body in attractive and stylish clothes. For some reason we feel more confident, more accepting of our bodies, when we dress in clothes that fit us and feel attractive.

We can ensure that our bodies function well so that we can walk, run, ski, dance, and make love with enjoyment.

We can eat regularly without guilt so that food is a normal part of life and no longer a moral issue. We can assess our emotional lives so that we do not use food to mask the problems that we do not want to face or that are too painful to face. We can find a therapist, a nutritionist, a support group who accept us, understand us, and can help.

b. FAMILY AND FRIENDS

1. At home and at work

Once a women accepts herself, how can she deal with the prejudice around her? Slowly, with attention to details, to remarks, articles, newspapers, movies, and jokes.

We can reach out into our families and refuse to accept their prejudiced views as reasonable or right.

"I disagree. Her problem is not that she is fat but that she didn't get the promotion."

"Her size has nothing to do with her competence."

"I'm not voting for her size, but for her grasp of what matters to women in this country."

We can discourage the behavior that comes from a belief in a narrow feminine ideal. We can discourage dieting, starving, and obsessive exercise.

We can refuse to talk about dieting in social conversations with our family and our friends. We can refuse to waste time talking about diets and weight loss. We can refuse to participate in the process of putting ourselves down.

2. The next generation

One of our greatest motivations for change is the concept that our daughters must not accept such a narrow definition of ideal. Our beautiful, talented, confident daughters must not feel flawed because they are not size ten. That motivation can send us to examine what our lives are telling our daughters.

Are we showing our daughters how to accept a natural weight? Of course not. Millions of women are dieting, and by dieting are telling their daughters that being feminine requires strict adherence to an external definition of normal, an external definition of ourselves, an external control over our lives. We have to change our own behavior if we want our daughters to change theirs. It is useless to tell your thirteen-year-old not to diet when she sees you skipping meals. We are leading by example, and we mothers are powerful leaders. How can we assure our daughters are free to be themselves?

If we diet, denigrate our bodies, complain about our weight, talk about "good" and "bad" foods, constantly strive for perfection, and see ourselves as worthwhile only if someone else approves of us, our daughters will probably believe that those attitudes are correct.

Women who are not mothers are also powerful examples to the young. An accomplished neighbor is a great influence on a teen. Her woman doctor is a great influence, as are her physics teacher, her school counselor, and her piano teacher. All the women a girl meets influence her. We are all showing her how we interpret what it means to be a woman.

But mothers are particularly influential. If a mother believes in the present social pressures on women and interprets them to her daughter as real and regulatory, then her daughter will accept society's restrictions as part of the price she pays for being born female.

Mothers' motivation for placing all this pressure on their daughters is usually one of caring and concern that their daughters be given all the opportunities that a size ten ideal women receives in this society. Many mothers are afraid that their daughters will not have opportunities, will not get into college, will not have friends, will not get married, will not feel confident, will not achieve, if they are not thin.

Such mothers believe that they are helping their daughters when they urge them to diet. They don't seem to see that they are increasing the pressures on their girls. Not only does a daughter have to fight the pressures of a skewed society, she has to resist the even stronger pressure of a mother who exaggerates those pressures in a dangerous example and an almost constant implied criticism of the daughter's appearance.

It would help if such mothers sat down with their daughters and explained how they were caught up in the media-designed world of size ten, how they regret the time, money, and effort chasing the impossible size, how it affects their relationships and their ambitions. They need to explain that they wish for a better, more realistic, broader world for their daughters.

It would help daughters to be able to talk about how they feel about the pressures of society, what they feel those pressures to be.

It would help daughters if mothers and daughters could talk about the options available to them, what would happen in their lives if they changed their attitudes toward themselves. Mothers and daughters may have different attitudes, different pressures, different options, but they could help each other to choose to be themselves, to choose to "write their own story," to become their own person, to be unique and individual.

They could gain mutual support from such a frank discussion. They need to show respect for each other's opinions, assessments, and choices. They need to encourage each other to make the choices that seem best. They need to allow each other to make mistakes in their choices, to suffer the consequences of those mistakes, to try again.

They need to explore the social world around them together looking at what does affect them, what does not, what they can change, what they cannot. The discussion should be an on-going exploration of how they feel, what they want, and how the world affects them. Each may have a different view and that must be acceptable. We are not looking for cloning here, just understanding and help.

Mothers can help their daughters but not if they pursue a double standard, believing size ten is good for mother, and any size is good for daughter. Young women will not accept that. In order to help the next generation, we must first deal with our own weight prejudice and our own slavish compliance with social pressures. It may be enough to express dissatisfaction, concern, and curiosity about the impossible pressures on us and around us. Most daughters would consider such concern and curiosity an indication of good intentions and be interested. You don't have to solve all your problems with body image before you can help your daughter with hers. But you must at least question the status quo.

We have responsibilities to ourselves and to each other to change how we deal with the oppression of weight prejudice. In changing ourselves, we are changing the next generation. We can't start soon enough.

Use the suggestions and checklists in Worksheet #6 as a starting point for mother and daughter discussions about body image.

Worksheet #7 has more suggestions for discussing weight and shape problems with your partner.

WORKSHEET #6
HELPING YOUR DAUGHTER CHANGE
HER ATTITUDE TOWARD HER BODY

First, you must seriously consider the messages you send your daughter, consciously and unconsciously. If you grab your stomach as you go past a mirror and grimace, your daughter will not believe that her less-than-perfect body is acceptable either.

Start by examining your own attitudes about your body. Talk to your daughter about your problems and your attitudes. Discuss her attitudes only if she offers them.

Explain to your daughter —

1. how your body image has crippled your self-esteem

2. how you have responded to media pressure to conform

3. how you are beginning to understand how that attitude enslaves you

4. how far you have to go to change your attitude

5. what role models inspire you — who in your life or in public life seems to accept herself and is admirable

6. how you started with a wonderful body that worked well and was attractive and how social pressures made you begin to believe that you were not good enough

7. how much time and money that attitude cost you: work out how much, over the years, this attitude cost you

8. how much it cost in friendships and relationships

9. how you are only now coming to realize what you have done to yourself

10. what plans you are making to change your attitude and increase your acceptance of your body

11. how you are trying to remove all "put downs" and derogatory remarks about your body from your conversation

13. that you need her help not to discuss diets, and not put down yourself or other people for their size or weight

Do not criticize her or suggest that she must do the same. She has to come to accept her body in her own time. You can show her what the problem is like for you and what you are trying to do about it, but you cannot make her decisions about her body for her. You can refuse to support any derogatory remarks about her body and object to any activity that contributes to making her feel as though her body is inadequate. Your daughter is far more likely to do as you do than to do as you say.

On the other hand, if you have an accepting attitude to your body but your daughter is ready to trade hers in, you might try talking to her about it.

1. Ask her how she feels about her body.

2. Ask her what her goals are. Are they possible, reasonable, healthy?

3. Discuss the set theory of weight; that she is more likely to achieve a stable weight with three regular, modest meals a day than yo-yo dieting.

4. Discuss the economic drive behind the social need to be thin.

5. Ask her how much time and money she is willing to spend on changing herself.

6. Ask her what she expects to achieve with change.

7. Point out that not accepting herself results in low self-esteem. Is that what she expects?

8. Ask her how you can help.

9. Do not offer solutions.

10. Do not offer to take charge.

11. Do not tell her she has to change.

12. Do not criticize the way she is.

13. Above all, listen to her.

I am not confident that you can change your partner's attitude. It may change in response to changes your make in yourself, but your partner may have a strong need to stay the same.

Education

1. Explain the set theory of weight.

2. Explain the economic drive behind the pursuit of thinness.

3. Explain the effects of dieting on the body.

4. Explain the failure rate of diets and the resulting increase in weight.

5. Explain the costs in time, money, and emotions.

Power struggle

Some partners need control. They use their unaccepting attitude toward your body as a way to keep you constantly off-balance, constantly trying to please. You probably won't be able to educate such partners since they do not want you to accept yourself.

1. Do not talk about weight and food. Talk about feelings.

2. Respond to their derogatory remarks about your body by labelling your feelings.

3. Work with a counselor to identify what is going on underneath your partner's efforts to control you. Try to work through those underlying problems.

4. Realize that your size, weight, and eating habits are not the problem here.

5. Some women find a friend or a parent in this power struggle position. Again, get help from a counselor.

Check whether you have a need to dominate others. Look at your relationships. Are you trying to dominate your daughter or your son by criticizing her or his body size?

c. CHANGING SOCIETY'S ATTITUDES

1. Organization

It is difficult to dismantle the vast diet industry with its thousands of institutions, weight clinics, and spas organized like a religion to convince, control, and condemn women. Such institutions are motivated by profit, a substantial motive, to maintain the present prejudice. As long as 92 percent of women are convinced they are overweight, there are potential customers. It benefits the diet, weight loss, and fitness industries to continue to convince the majority of the population that they are not good enough and need the products or services offered for sale. We can change this, but it is a big job.

Most people with a more realistic attitude to weight are not organized to combat this prejudice. They don't stand on street corners and preach. They don't organize "Anti-weight Watchers". They don't set up community clinics. They don't even protest much when people make prejudiced remarks.

Some people are getting angry and concerned enough to get organized. A group in Toronto, Canada, called HER SIZE was formed to fight shape and weight prejudice. It wages a letter and article writing campaign to confront weight prejudice where it occurs. These women have made changes in local papers as well as in *The New York Times*.

This group, with the cooperation of the public health department and Toronto school personnel, has also designed and implemented a weight and shape education program that attempts to educate students about weight prejudice in our society and the restricting, limiting results of such prejudice. In order to make this educational program work, the educators had to begin with the nurses and teachers involved in the program. Nurses in particular seem to have a great degree of weight prejudice and must consciously work to understand and change their attitudes.

Other groups have formed to celebrate big bodies, to actively promote the well-being of large men and women, or to fight weight and shape prejudice. Organizations exist to help those with eating disorders (see Appendix 2). Magazines, including *Radiance Magazine*, exist to help large women find role models, information, and support (see the bibliography).

One of the quickest ways to elicit change is to build in a profit for an industry. Energetic entrepreneurs need to see the advantage of varied body size in terms of dollars and cents. Millions of women not size ten represent a sizable buying public. But few sales and marketing programs exist to service those buyers.

If we react against ads that idealize size ten or that ridicule variations of body size and boycott products that advertise size ten as "average" and "ideal," we can make our point economically where it is likely to get the most corporate attention. Lower sales would force different advertising.

2. Education

It may take people without weight prejudice in influential positions in manufacturing companies to turn the tide of sales promotion. It may take people who understand the problem of weight prejudice to change advertising, sales, and retail buying. If people in these sections of industry understand weight prejudice, they could refuse to accept our social ideals and make changes.

We need TV and film writers and producers to break away from the present stereotypes. Cartoonists need to stop representing large women as failures. Once the change begins it will grow until it is truly permanent.

Education makes for lasting changes. We must educate others about the facts of weight issues and the errors of present myths. We can write letters to the editor when we see weight prejudice in the newspaper. We can deal directly with the prejudice of others, with the fears of employers that we will be unhealthy and miss work, that we will be unable to deal with the public, that we will be slow at the job.

We can fight the size ten ideal in thousands of small decisions: telling a sales clerk that our bodies are fine, her clothes are too small, refusing to diet, refusing to talk about dieting.

Perhaps the only effective way we have to make changes is to convey through letters, books, and our individual attitudes the conviction that such prejudice is ignorant, that men and women of intelligence, the bright people, the "with-it" crowd do not indulge in shape and weight prejudice.

There are changes happening in social acceptance of the ubiquitous size ten. Talented large women are writing books in protest, giving examples of the hardships they have suffered and their solutions to some of the problems. *Breaking All the Rules*, by Nancy Roberts, is a good example. Researchers such as Janet Polivy and C. Peter Herman (in

Breaking the Diet Habit: the Natural Weight Alternative) are taking a more positive approach.

We also need the backing of big business executives and sales staff. We need women who understand the oppression of our present social standards to be in positions in industry to make changes. We need role models of various shapes and weights in film, in politics, and in all careers, as evidence of our success. We need to have a more realistic, reasonable, commonsense attitude to our bodies. It is up to women to make those attitudes accepted and commonplace.

It is possible to make social changes without protest marches and violent attacks on the status quo, but it is hard to make social changes without educating others and without commitment by individuals. Women need to understand the nature of the oppression that society decrees with weight and shape stereotypes. We need to understand how that restricts our lives. We need to be committed to change.

What every woman must understand is that the answer to weight prejudice is not diet. The answer is not to force everyone to be thin. The answer is not in restructuring the shape of the individual woman. The answer is in restructuring society's concept of what is normal.

EPILOGUE

We are different one from another. We expect to be different races, different religions, hold different ideologies, have different educations status, different levels of intelligence, different colored hair, eyes, skin. We expect to grow to different heights. Why, then, do we think we all have to be the same weight?

We are wonderfully different, and within those differences we can develop interesting, productive, and powerful personalities. We do not need the oppression of the narrow body image to restrict us. We need more freedom of size and shape, more ability to be what is natural to us.

You have read this book, and, I hope, thought about it, thought about what it means in your own life, in your family, in your community. Read the lists of books in the bibliography, the lists of organizations that might help you. Take out a subscription to an inspiring magazine such as *Radiance Magazine,* talk to other women, talk to your daughters, your mother, your friends. Consider what weight prejudice means in your life.

Write to me if you wish, and tell me about it. I'm not writing to my computer or my publisher, I'm writing to you and I'd like to hear from you. Write to me at this address:

Marion Crook
c/o Self-Counsel Press
1704 N. State Street
Bellingham, WA 98225

or

Self-Counsel Press
1481 Charlotte Road
North Vancouver, B.C.
Canada V7J 1H1

If you want me to speak to your group, write and tell me about the plans you are making.

We can make a difference. I have faith in the collective common sense of most women. Once they are aware of the social manipulation to keep them thin, the media persuasion, the crippling effects of the diet industry, they will — we will — refuse to be intimidated, refuse to be pushed, refuse to be victimized by a socially distorted body image. We will celebrate our differences; we will accept and enjoy our differences; and we will develop a healthy, individual body image.

APPENDIX 1
CANADA'S FOOD GUIDE

For an adult (non-nursing, not pregnant)

Group Portions per day

- Milk and milk products 2 servings
- Meat, fish, poultry and alternates(eggs, beans) 2 servings
- Breads and cereals 3–5 servings
- Fruits and vegetables 4–5 servings

Examples of one serving

- Milk and milk products
- 1 serving = 250 ml (1 cup) milk
- 45 g (1½ ounces) cheddar or processed cheese
- Meat and alternates 1 serving = 60–90 g (2–3 ounces) cooked lean meat
- 60 ml (4 tbsp) peanut butter
- 250 ml (1 cup) cooked dried peas or lentils
- 2 eggs

Breads and cereals

- 1 serving = 1 slice bread
- 125 ml (½ cup) cooked cereal
- 175 ml (¾ cup) ready-to-eat cereal
- ½ hamburger or wiener bun

Fruits and vegetables

- 1 serving = 125 ml (½ cup) vegetables or fruits — fresh, frozen, or canned
- 1 medium-sized potato, carrot, tomato, apple, orange, or banana

Taken from Canada's Food Guide Handbook (Revised), Health and Welfare Canada, ISBN 0-662-11947-9

APPENDIX 2
ADDRESSES

National Association of Anorexia Nervosa
    and Associated Diseases
Box 7
Highland Park, Illinois
60035
(708) 831-3438

National Anorexic Aid Society
1925 East Dublin/Granville Road
Columbus, Ohio
43229
(613) 426-1112

National Eating Disorders Information Centre
Toronto General Hospital
CW1-325, 200 Elizabeth St.
Toronto, Ontario
Canada
(416) 340-4156

BIBLIOGRAPHY

PERIODICALS

Magazines

BBW (Big Beautiful Woman)
  Box 16958
  North Hollywood, California
  91615-9964

Radiance Magazine
  Box 30246
  Oakland, California
  94604

Academic articles

Bauer, Barbara G., and Wayne P. Anderson. "In the Field: Bulimic Beliefs, Food for Thought." *Journal of Counseling and Development* 67 (March 1989): 416.

Cooper, Stewart E. "Chemical Dependency and Eating Disorders: Are They So Different?" *Journal of Counseling and Development* (Sept./Oct. 1989).

Dejong, William. "The Stigma of Obesity: The Consequences of Naive Assumptions Concerning the Causes of Physical Deviance." *Journal of Health and Social Behavior* 21 (March 1980): 75–87.

Gladis, Madeline M., and B. Timothy Walsh. "Premenstrual Exacerbation of Binge Eating in Bulimia." *American Journal of Psychiatry* 144 (1987): 1592.

Goldner, Elliott, and Susan Leung. "Anorexia and Bulimia Nervosa: Outpatient Management." *B.C. Medical Journal*, vol. 31, no. 5 (May 1989): 279–280.

Manley, Ronald S. "Anorexia and Bulimia Nervosa: Psychological Features, Assessment, and Treatment." *B.C. Medical Journal*, vol. 31, no. 3 (March 1989): 151–154.

Marazziti, Donatella, Elena Macchi, Alessandro Rotondo, Giani Franco Placidi, and Giovanni B. Cassano. "Involvement of Serotonin System in Bulimia." *Life Sciences* 4: 2123–2126.

Phelan, Kelly, et al. "Premenstrual Exacerbation of Binge Eating in Bulimia." *American Journal of Psychiatry* 48 (1986): 415–422.

Yates, Alayne. "Current Perspectives on the Eating Disorders: I. History, Psychological and Biological Aspects." *Journal of the American Academy of Child Adolescent Psychiatry*, vol. 28, no. 6 (1989): 813–828.

Yates, Alayne. "Current Perspectives on the Eating Disorders: II. Treatment, Outcome and Research Directions." *Journal of the American Academy of Child Adolescent Psychiatry*, vol. 29, no. 1 (1990): 1–9.

BOOKS

Bolen, Jean Shinoda. *Goddesses in Every Woman: A New Psychology of Women*. New York: Harper Colophon books, Harper and Row, 1984.

Bruch, Hilde. *Conversations with Anorexics*. New York: Basic Books Inc., 1988.

Bruch, Hilde. *The Golden Cage: The Enigma of Anorexia Nervosa*. Cambridge, MA: Harvard University Press, 1978.

Brumberg, Joan Jacobs. *Fasting Girls: The Emergence of Anorexia Nervoxa as a Modern Disease*. Cambridge, MA: Harvard University Press, 1988.

Byrne, Katerine. *A Parent's Guide to Anorexia and Bulimia*. New York: Schocken Books, 1987.

Cannon, Geoffrey, and Hetty Einzig. *Stop Dieting Because Dieting Makes You Fat*. New York: Simon and Schuster, 1985.

Chernin, Kim. *The Obsession: Reflections on the Tyranny of Slenderness*. New York: Harper and Row, 1981.

Davidson, Joy. *The Agony of it All: The Drive for Drama and Excitement in Women's Lives*. Los Angeles: Jeremy P. Tarcher Inc., 1988.

Freedman, Rita Jackaway. *Body Image: Learning to Like Our Looks and Ourselves*. New York: Harper, 1988.

Garfinkel, Paul E., and David M. Garner. *Anorexia Nervosa: A Multidimensional Perspective*. New York: Brunner/Mazel Publishers, 1982.

Heilbrun, Carolyn G. *Writing a Woman's Life*. New York: Ballantine Books, 1988.

Jasper, Karin. *Are You Too Fat, Ginny?* Toronto: Is Five Press, 1988.

Johnson, C. and M. E. Commors. *The Etiology and Treatment of Bulimia Nervosa: A Biopsychosocial Perspective*. New York: Basic Books, 1987.

Lawrence, Marilyn. *The Anorexic Experience*. London: The Women's Press Handbook Series, 1984/85.

McCoy, Kathleen. *Coping with Teenage Depression*. New York and Scarborough, Ontario: New American Library, 1982

Malone, Thomas Patrick, and Patrick Thomas Malone. *The Art of Intimacy*. New York: Prentice Hall, 1987.

Millman, Marcia. *Such a Pretty Face: Being Fat in America*. New York: W.W. Norton Co., 1980.

Orbach, Susan. *Fat is a Feminist Issue II*. New York: Berkley Books, 1982.

Overeaters Annonymous. *Overeaters Annonymous*. Torrance, California: 1980.

Polivy, J., and C.P. Herman. *Breaking the Diet Habit: The Natural Weight Alternative*. New York: Basic Books Inc., 1983.

Price, Susan. *The Hidden Ego: The Hidden Power Women Possess But Are Afraid to Use*. New York: Rawson Assoc., 1984.

Roberts, Nancy. *Breaking All the Rules: Feeling Good and Looking Great No Matter What Your Size*. New York: Viking Penguin, 1985.

Roth, Geneen. *Breaking Free From Compulsive Eating*. New York: Penguin, 1984.

Schwartz, Hillel. *Never Satisfied: A Cultural History of Diets, Fantasies and Fat*. New York: Macmillan, 1986.

Showalter, Elaine. *The Female Malady: Women, Madness and English Culture, 1830-1980*. New York: Penguin Books, 1985.

Szekely, Eva. *Never Too Thin*. Toronto: The Women's Press, 1988.

Valette, Bret. *A Parent's Guide to Eating Disorders, Prevention and Treatment of Anorexia Nervosa and Bulimia*. New York: Walker Publishing Co., 1988.

Vipond, Mary. *The Mass Media in Canada*. Toronto: James Lorimer & Co., 1989.

Walsh, Mary Roth, ed. *The Psychology of Women: Ongoing Debates.* New Haven, London: Yale University Press, 1987.

Wolman, Benyamin B. *Psychological Aspects of Obesity, A Handbook.* New York: Van Nostrand Reinhold Co., 1982.

Woodman, Marion. *The Owl Was a Baker's Daughter.* Toronto: Inner City Books, 1980.

REPORTS AND PAMPHLETS

Brown, Catrina. *Getting Beyond Weight: Women Helping Women.* Women's Health Clinic, Winnipeg.

Garner, D. M., M. P. Olmstead, and J. Polivy. *Eating Disorders Inventory (EDI).* Psychological Assessment Resource, 1984.

Goldner, E. M. *Body Image Test.* St. Paul's Hospital Eating Disorders Clinic, Vancouver.

Health Promotion and Counseling for Youth, Saskatchewan Health. *Food, Fitness and Feelings: An Activity Learning Guide for Youth Group Leaders and Teachers.* Community Health Services, Regina, 1979.

Health Promotion Directorate. *Canadian Guidelines for Healthy Weights.* Health and Welfare Canada, 1988.

Health Services and Protection Branch. *Promoting Healthy Weights: A Discussion Paper.* National Health and Welfare Canada, 1988.

Health and Welfare Canada. *Canada's Guidelines for Healthy Eating.* Supply and Services Canada, 1990.

Health and Welfare Canada. *Canada's Food Guide Handbook.* Supply and Services Canada, 1987.

McCreary Centre Society. *The Provincial Task Force Eating Disorder Report.* Vancouver, 1989.

U.S. Department of Agriculture, U.S. Deparment of Health and Human Services. *Nutrition and Your Health: Dietary Guidelines for Americans.* 1990.

FURTHER READING

Hutchinson, Marcia Germain. *Transforming Body Image, New York.* New York: Crossing Press, 1985.

Kano, Susan. *Making Peace With Food.* New York: Harper and Row, 1989.

Sandbek, Terence. *Deadly Diet: Recovering from Anorexia and Bulimia.* Oakland: New Harvinger Inc., 1986.

Sandford, Linda T., and Mary Ellen Donovan. *Women and Self-Esteem.* New York: Penguin, 1984.

Schoenfielder, Lisa, and Barb Wieser, eds. *Shadow on a Tightrope: Writings by Women on Fat Oppression.* Iowa City: Women's Press, 1983.